Transgender Justice in Schools

EDITORS Linda Christensen AND Ty Marshall

A RETHINKING SCHOOLS PUBLICATION

Transgender Justice in Schools
Edited by Linda Christensen and Ty Marshall

A Rethinking Schools Publication

Rethinking Schools, Ltd., is a nonprofit educational publisher of books, booklets, and a quarterly magazine on school reform, with a focus on issues of equity and social justice. To request additional copies of this book or a catalog of other publications, or to subscribe to *Rethinking Schools* magazine, contact:

Rethinking Schools
6737 W. Washington St., Suite 3249
Milwaukee, Wisconsin 53214
800-669-4192
www.rethinkingschools.org

Cover/Book Design: Nancy Zucker
Cover Illustration: Micah Bazant
Curriculum Editor: Bill Bigelow
Proofreading: Lawrence Sanfilippo
Index: Heather Dubnick

ISBN: 978-0-942961-46-1

Library of Congress Control Number: 2024941370

CONTENTS

CHAPTER FOUR: FIGHTING FOR THE RIGHT TO TEACH

CHAPTER FIVE: RESOURCES

INTRODUCTION

TRANSGENDER JUSTICE IN SCHOOLS

Officials across the country — from governors to legislators to school superintendents — have marshaled anti-LGBTQ+ laws banning gender-affirming care for transgender youth, requiring or allowing the misgendering of trans students in schools, instituting "bathroom bills" that discriminate against trans youth, censoring teachers from teaching LGBTQ+ or critical race theory curriculum, and banning books by and about LGBTQ+ and BIPOC people, constructing an atmosphere of fear and intolerance in schools. We crafted *Transgender Justice in Schools* as an act of solidarity to uplift the work of students, teachers, parents, and communities who refuse to be silenced by this legislative war against trans kids.

In their article, "Teaching Them into Existence," Mykhiel Deych wrote, "Teaching isn't supposed to include life-or-death consequences, but it does. When it comes to LGBTQ+ students, we fail to hold space for their existence. Heterocentric, cisnormative curriculum writes out the existence of LGBTQ+ lives. Campaigns such as Dan Savage's 'It Gets Better' go viral precisely because we aren't actually reassuring youth that their existence is acceptable, real, normal. We need an 'It Gets Better' campaign because high school is awful for LGBTQ kids, high school is fatal."

Nex Benedict, a nonbinary 10th grader and member of the Choctaw Nation, died after a fight in the high school bathroom that Oklahoma lawmakers forced them to use. Benedict's death underscores the life-or-death consequences for nonbinary students when lawmakers play politics with their lives. Oklahoma Gov. Kevin Stitt has signed more than 50 anti-gay bills, like the ones requiring students to use bathrooms that match their sex assigned at birth, banning the use of nonbinary gender markers on IDs, restricting gender-affirming care, and banning transgender girls from participating in girls' sports. As Freedom Oklahoma, an LGBTQ advocacy group, noted, "Whether Nex died as a direct result of injuries sustained in the brutal hate-motivated attack at school or not, Nex's death is a result of being the target of physical and emotional harm because of who Nex was."

Lawmakers have targeted teachers as well. School districts across the country are firing teachers, like Melissa Tempel, for standing up against the anti-gay legislation. For every teacher fired or reprimanded or mandated to exclude LGBTQ+ studies or take down the rainbow on their classroom wall, there are hundreds, maybe thousands, who are too scared or feel too unprepared to teach about LGBTQ+ issues. We created this book to bridge the gap between where we are as educators and where we need to be.

In an interview with Ali Velshi on MSNBC's *Velshi Banned Book Club*, Alex Gino, author of the trans book, *Melissa* (formerly published as *George*), spoke about the need for schools to step up:

> School is the place where [students] can get information, where they can figure out who they are and who other people are. If we don't do that, what you end up with is adults who are either hurt and scarred or they don't know how to interact with a trans person. That's where you get epidemic levels of violence against trans people, particularly trans women of color. This attempt to protect children is actually putting people at risk. Information saves lives and books save lives.

Every teacher, administrator, counselor, college professor, school board member, or parent has a moral obligation to figure out how to use their knowledge and privilege to increase support for trans students and teachers.

CHAPTER 1: IT'S A MATTER OF LIFE AND DEATH

We named the first chapter of *Transgender Justice in Schools* "It's a Matter of Life and Death" — because it is. In this chapter, trans teachers, writers, and the parent of a trans child discuss the fear, danger, and loneliness trans people experience in schools. Maximillian Matthews, a writer from Durham, North Carolina, wrote about trans students' suicides in their article "How We Failed Nigel Shelby and Allowed the Abuse He Endured." Matthews underscores how curricular silence functions to isolate trans students, especially trans students of color, which can lead to suicide.

> I longed to read about someone who was attracted to men like I was. I longed to see someone who rejected the labels assigned to them as I struggled to do. There was a time when all I wanted was a confirmation I was not alone in my queerness.
>
> Despite the few examples that existed as I grew up in the '90s, the isolation I felt led me to consider suicide. In my mind, death was better

> than loneliness. Tragically, I was already battling a system that determined conservatism was better than queerness, normalcy better than diversity, conformity better than nonconformity, and whiteness better than Blackness. This was the system that decided what I did and did not see, what received approval and what did not, and whose life had value and whose did not. It was a system constructed to intentionally exclude, oppress, marginalize, and eradicate people like me and Nigel Shelby.

In *Transgender Justice in Schools*, we want to illuminate the dire social emergency that both Deych and Matthews write about and the life and death consequences for the trans and BIPOC communities. We also want to acknowledge the need to move beyond subjects of fear and rejection and demonstrate the existence of queer joy as Ty Marshall wrote in their piece "Becoming Unapologetically Trans":

> I want to show students what steady self-love in the face of fear looks like, because we will all face it. I want to teach my students that being trans means continuing to live into our joy — and express our full selves despite backlash. The room I make for myself cracks at the rigidity and makes room for others — by surviving we protect each other from the resurgence of transphobia. My lesson in personhood is that we cannot turn on ourselves when the world is already turning on us. . . . A teacher in their full humanity and power can recognize the same in their students, and demand better from the education system that dehumanizes all of us.

In fact, a world filled with "steady self-love" should be far easier to create than the one where legislators write laws that encourage others to bully children, like Nex Benedict, who want nothing more than a chance to live in the "full humanity" Ty Marshall describes.

CHAPTER 2: TEACHING TRANS CURRICULUM

We understand that many teachers don't know where to begin when teaching LGBTQ+ curriculum because few schools or universities have modeled the inclusion of intersectional queer studies. In "Teaching Them into Existence," Mykhiel Deych asked us the questions that we all need to figure out:

> How many LGBTQ authors do you teach about? How often is the intersection and difference of sexuality and gender addressed in your Socratic seminars? Do you discuss transgender history in U.S. history? Do you reveal authors' struggles with sexuality and how these relate to their art? Has gay culture ever been given the credit it deserves for spurring numerous fashion, music, and art trends? No, and me neither. As an out trans and gay teacher I can't always fend off the fear of a parental uprising about my "gay agenda." This sort of bravery hasn't yet materialized in my classroom, but I'm working on it.

In Chapter 2, "Teaching Trans Curriculum," teachers across content areas and grade levels attempt to answer Deych's questions by demonstrating theoretical positions, units, and strategies to pave the way for educators looking for how to build a more inclusive curriculum.

In "Queering Black History and Getting Free," Dominique Hazzard challenges teachers to rethink the way history is written and who is represented. "I am a queer Black woman. By this I mean that my sexuality exists outside the margins, between the approved boundaries, beyond the limits of most imaginations. A queer thing is a thing that existing words cannot yet adequately describe, a thing that our language and our boxes have not yet evolved to capture. So, what does queering something mean? To me it means turning the thing on its head: questioning its assumed narratives, reworking its categories, and upending its status quo. Let's queer Black history." Hazzard's article is an invitation to turn our work on its head, to question our old narratives and ways of teaching.

In the same chapter, Sam Long whose article "Diversity Is What Makes It Interesting to Study Living Things" demonstrates how he has upended the status quo in his high school biology class by discussing gender diversity, disrupting students' assumptions about the complexities of gender. "By talking about gender diversity in our classrooms, we can engage minds, de-pathologize difference, cultivate empathy, and support academic rigor for all." Long rejects the notion that teachers lack the time to teach about gender diversity: "The biology classroom has more than enough room to include and celebrate all genders. Like most teachers, I feel the pressure to get through my curriculum and prepare for standardized tests. But when I teach about the complexities of gender, I generate authentic student engagement that drives learning throughout the year."

Queering curriculum is not just a favor teachers do for LGBTQ+ students. A queer curriculum offers a fuller, more comprehensive curriculum for all students. As students in Linda Christensen's lesson on anti-gay laws noted, "Part of the importance of [*Melissa*] is getting a trans person's perspective about what they go through, what they are sometimes forced to hide about themselves. If you don't have that perspective, non-trans students get sheltered from trans people's lives. If you don't understand something, it makes it hard for you to appreciate someone else's struggle. We need these stories that are important for trans kids to have, but for non-trans kids too."

CHAPTER 3: TRANS STUDENTS SPEAK OUT

In the third chapter, "Trans Students Speak Out," we connected with trans students to share their insights about schools. We asked them two questions: What actions have teachers/schools taken to make you feel supported and welcome — in the classroom, the curriculum, the school? And: What other changes do teachers/schools need to make for trans students/teachers to feel supported and welcome — in the classroom, the curriculum, the school?

Although most student responses came from schools, districts, and states that offer some protection, like GSAs and gender-neutral bathrooms — even laws mandating LGBTQ+ curriculum — students still struggle. Bullying continues, especially for trans students. The wise words of the students we interviewed speak of the many ways educators and systems need to do better, but they also point us in the direction of change. None of these students had to endure the anti-LGBTQ+ laws that Nex Benedict encountered in Oklahoma or that students face in other states like Florida, Georgia, Missouri, Nebraska, or West Virginia.

While many students praised their schools and teachers for sorting out their names and pronouns and making them feel seen and safe in schools, others reported the difficulty of getting teachers to simply use their preferred names and pronouns:

> As a trans person, just the act of seeing or hearing my deadname is enough to make me upset. And I know this is a common feeling within the community. Many students do not have a safe place in their lives in which they have the luxury to change a given name. It's a part of ourselves we have grown out of, and hearing it is an act of disrespect to our identity. In class, specifically when there are substitute teachers, I get extreme anxiety knowing that my deadname will be read aloud during attendance. The act of having to tell the substitute the specific situation and why, is incredibly scary for a student who does not feel comfortable with the person they are sharing it with. This is causing students to out themselves in situations they may not be comfortable with, and often in front of all their peers.

Most students could not rustle up many — or any — examples of LGBTQ+ curriculum in their schools. A student from Philadelphia wrote, "Since coming out as nonbinary, I haven't really felt seen in most of my classes, and I even had to struggle through a class in which a teacher constantly mocked trans women and had us debate whether trans women should be allowed in women's sports (terrifyingly, most of the class said they shouldn't be allowed)."

However, that same student, now enrolled in a Queer History class, wrote things are better this year. Their shout-out to their English teacher provides insights for how the changes educators make matter: "I also appreciate that my English teacher, after learning that I am nonbinary, saw how it related to our topics that we are learning about in the class and pointed out how gender fluidity and being trans break the constraints of expectations and stereotypes (something we were studying earlier in the year). I do wish that more teachers would bring queerness and queer topics into their lessons, like if standard history classes could also mention queer history." A number of students pointed out that LGBTQ+ students should not be called on to address or answer questions about their identities in class.

Students also found acceptance and joy in school. As a student from Massachusetts wrote, "Luckily 6th grade opened up a new world of queerness. I connected with so many gay and queer people and met a couple nonbinary people, who helped me discover that that's who I felt I was. They had this thing called GSA that was all about the LGBTQIAP+ community and I no longer felt alone."

CHAPTER 4: FIGHTING FOR THE RIGHT TO TEACH

In *A Trans History: Time Marches Forward and So Do We.*, a beautiful documentary by Chase Strangio and Zackary Drucker about trans history, narrator Laverne Cox says, "Try as they might, these lawmakers can't erase us. Our rights will be hard-won, but we are winning. Following in the footsteps of Flawless, Major, Sylvia, Marsha, we fight back the way they did. We take care of each other. We tell our stories. And we demand justice. Our community is resilient, and our history of resistance runs deep. Resistance is our birthright, the gift passed from our elders."

The fourth chapter of *Transgender Justice in Schools* highlights the stories of educators who follow in the footsteps of the trans elders this documentary celebrates. Melissa Tempel spoke out in the media about her district's discriminatory practices; Julianna Iacovelli decided to be open and out in school. "It allows me to be some form of representation and to show that we are here in every community. . . . Being nonbinary in the classroom is not just a struggle, it's a superpower and I wanted the school I chose to support that."

In "Big Reactions to Small Steps: One Teacher's Story About Using Inclusive Children's Literature," Nettie Harrington Pangallo tells the story of answering a 2nd-grade student's question "What does gay mean?" in a rural community in central Virginia. "[M]y first thought was that my administration would expect me not to answer the question and refer the child to their parents. I also knew that this was why it was important to address it, particularly when the student revealed that another student had been calling children gay at recess. Avoiding the question would send a strong message to my students. I decided to address it." When parents objected to her lessons, Pangallo stood strong, gathering support from teachers and community members as well as from national organizations. She wrote:

> [W]e can push back on policies, prejudice, and "remaining neutral." By engaging in one-on-one conversations in our schools and partnering with local and national social justice organizations, we can work toward a curriculum that honors children's natural curiosity and the healthy expression of diversity within our communities. Engaging students in conversation through inclusive literature is a small, but important step.

We produced this book as an act of defiance. While lawmakers attempt to delete queer people from the curriculum and the libraries, from health care and bathrooms, we resist. We refuse to accept their unjust laws. And we encourage others to refuse as well. We must protect our students who come out and take up space and demand their chosen names be spoken with the reverence due their rebirth. We must gather to fight alongside educators, parents and community members who build safe and welcoming harbors within educational spaces. As *Rethinking Schools* editors wrote, "Every action we take in schools to welcome those who have been traditionally marginalized reminds us that we are doing this work for all of us, helping all of us become better human beings. ●

CHAPTER ONE

A MATTER OF LIFE AND DEATH

LISTEN
CELEBRATING TRANSGENDER STUDENTS
LOVE
ARN
EBIN LEE

BECOMING UNAPOLOGETICALLY TRANS

BY TY MARSHALL

To Whom It May Concern:
I, ___Laura Taylor__ am transitioning from female to male and will now be known as __Tyler Marshall___. I give the district permission to share this information, and I understand I am encouraged not to discuss this transition, gender identity, or sexual orientation during instructional time.

I had been called to a meeting to "discuss my transition" with the head of human resources and my principal after coming out to her — after almost a year of living a double life. I was Ty at home and Laura at school, the "Ms. Taylor" stinging and making me shrink into myself, students' confusion and the incredulous "You're Ms. Taylor?!" As students laughed, I almost felt relieved that they were willing to acknowledge what no adults in the majority white, suburban, wealthy, and conservative Christian community where I taught would — at least I was not invisible to them.

I remember looking across the table at the union rep — a caring old white guy who just shrugged and said, "I think you should sign this." I wish I could say I resisted, but I did not. Under our district letterhead, like some sort of policy memo, were the facts about my identity printed carefully, and a clear message — *my* life is not a valuable part of "instructional time." I signed it. I was near the end of my first year of teaching, swimming in all kinds of self-doubt about my practice, and self-doubt about how the person I was could have room to exist in the place that I taught.

When I signed that paper, I signed away a lot of myself: my ability to build relationships with my students, to tell them simple stories about my day, my family, or my childhood. The school had sent my students a letter over the summer — "when they have time to process" — about my gender identity, but I was not allowed to discuss it with them the following fall. I became robo-teacher, tensely smiling and squeaking out "good" in my newly-on-testosterone voice when anyone asked me how my weekend was. One of the basic tenets of teaching is to embed the curriculum in students' lives, and to do that, teachers must demonstrate a willingness to share their lives. But I had a gag order: Who I was, my transition, my family was not to be a part of classroom instruction.

IMPACT OF SILENCE

My first-year teaching as Mr. Marshall was even more tense than the year before — students I had the previous year avoided my eyes. I remember smiling out into the hallways at my former students, and how they stared so hard ahead — the way you do when you are trying not to look at someone — and my smile would fall. I wonder who saw me in those moments.

Every interaction with students — in the classrooms, in the hallways, and in what parts of our lives we allow ourselves to share is "instructional time." As educator Jennifer Gonzalez, host of the *Cult of Pedagogy* podcast, explains:

> [The students] are watching. Every moment students spend in our rooms, amid the business of the day, the paper pushing and content coverage, amid the setup and teardown of projects, they hear everything we say. About ourselves. About the world. About them. They watch how we handle ourselves when we are pressed for time and when we receive gifts and when we screw things up. . . . Whatever it is we put before them, they will learn from it.

My gag order followed me like a screaming critic — "Don't say that" "That one's gonna cost ya." I was so busy policing my own movements I couldn't really connect with anyone. My second-year "instructional time" was fear-fog — mine and theirs. It was "Trans people are OK, as long as you keep them at a distance." I could walk around the building, even teach my classes, but not let down my guard.

I worked hard for a long time to program the moves of robo-teacher. If I could just deliver the information in the right way, develop the perfect curriculum, I could break through the fog. But students are smart; they hear silence on the things we are unwilling to name loud and clear. Our school's vision statement included a "caring, joyful, inclusive, and healthy learning community," but despite those words, students transferred out of my classes, parents examined my social media and filed complaints, and co-workers told me "Around here, you keep your social justice work under wraps so as not to get on anyone's radar."

Whelp, too late for that. My principal said at one point, "Don't worry, give it a few years and they won't even know." She hoped, I think, that I would magically turn into a tiny lumberjack, masculine and fist-bumping students — trans-erased.

The agreement I made followed me through my second, third, and fourth years as a teacher. Each year I thought, if I can just show a little more of my own life and whole self to my students, I can make more room for all of us — trans, queers, whatever kind of non-normative anything in the white suburbs of West Linn, Oregon.

MAKING ROOM FOR QUEER STUDENTS

An 8th grader at the end of my first year sought me out for "gender chats" before school. They eventually wrote a petition to start a group called SAGA (Sexuality and Gender Alliance), their parting gift they had asked for from administration for three years. We started with three students. The following year we ended with 20 — as students told each other about the group, and rushed in to fill the open space like water traveling over parched earth seeking an opening, a crack in the ground. They entered the classroom after school, threw down their bags, and started dancing — we always had a DJ, a nail station, some workshops on walking in heels. My third year, students organized a movie night to show *Love, Simon* and got censored by the administration for the three words in the movie that reference anal sex. But students doggedly worked around it to create a "GAY-me night" that was a huge success. The SAGA students ended the year with a Pride Picnic complete with rainbow cupcakes and a Billie Eilish dance party on the field with students wearing their trans and pride flags as capes. I felt like we had been victorious — we were bringing to bear what the administration would not allow me to address in instructional time.

The students teach what I cannot — this world has room for us, take up space and dance anyway.

We had gone from being tolerated to demanding acceptance. Tolerance is: You are allowed to be here. Tolerance is: You can be here but don't make too much of a fuss. My school's vision of "caring, joyful, inclusive learning communities" fell flat to our queer students. The student body tolerated our existence, and we could have a club, as long as we didn't make a fuss. Acceptance, on the other hand, is: You can be here and be your whole human self, and my world has room for you. The SAGA students teach what I cannot — this world has room for us, take up space and dance anyway. The lesson is: We are here. We will not wait for your instructional time to allow us in.

BACKLASH AND BETRAYAL

The students who were so deeply afraid were also not waiting. On the last day of school of my third year as a teacher, the 7th-grade boys were ready to step into their power as the rulers of the school now that the 8th graders had graduated and gone. I saw a bustle of activity in the classroom across the hall right before our 9:15 a.m. bell to start the day. Students moved quickly, in sync, with the powerful pull of groupthink.

I saw boys bumping chests in their eagerness to get in and out of the classroom. They grabbed the American flag hanging in the teacher's room, then filed out, kept moving, grabbing more flags as they passed each classroom. I heard the national anthem blaring on a Bluetooth speaker, playing from one of their cell phones. Several "Make America Great Again" hats dotted the gaggle of maybe 15 boys. I made eye contact with the teacher whose classroom they emerged from and got a worried shrug. Then the chanting started: "Two genders! Two genders! Two genders!"

My shock froze me for a second. The other teacher had been swallowed by her classroom again, probably trying to calm the 6th graders left behind in the wake. This couldn't be happening. My mind flashed to the Charlottesville news footage of white men marching against Black Lives Matter organizers with torches, chanting "Jews will not replace us . . ." as I started walking after them. My voice, still squeaky and weak from testosterone, barely reached over the national anthem. We made it to the library before I could slow them down.

"Hey gentlemen!"

They slowed, the few I knew from my own classes looked sideways avoiding my eyes. I hardly remembered what I said — something like: "This can't happen right now." Maybe I was thinking this can't happen here? Their response was immediate as they shook the American flags "borrowed" from many teachers' classrooms: "Well, how come they can have gay flags and we can't have these?"

How we treat ourselves is part of the "curriculum."

I was scared in front of all those boys. It feels silly to say about some excited 13-year-olds from a grown person. Not that they would hurt me, but I defaulted, recalling an earlier conversation with my vice principal where he asked me to tell the SAGA students not to wear their flags anymore — fearing a backlash just like this. I found his words coming out of my mouth, cotton-sticky like when you tell a lie. "No one is allowed to wear or carry anything that disrupts the learning environment. It's in the Constitution. Not even the SAGA kids."

My betrayal in this moment — of myself, my students — flattened any further interaction or possibility as I automo-tron-ically instructed them to put their flags away and head to class. I don't know why no other teachers joined in that moment; they were all busy in their classrooms readying the instructional time.

In this moment, I taught so many things I didn't want to teach. I taught them to push aside their feelings and go to class. I taught them that our learning environment does not include queer or trans visibility. I taught them, ultimately, that I was afraid of having the conversation with them, and that intimidation can get trans and queer people to put away their flags — to put away their identities.

No matter how we respond when we fall short of who we want to be, we are still teaching. How we treat ourselves is part of the "curriculum." I want to show students what steady self-love in the face of fear looks like, because we will all face it. I want to teach my students that being trans means continuing to live into our joy — and express our full selves despite backlash. The room I make for myself cracks at the rigidity and makes room for others — by surviving we protect each other from the resurgence of transphobia. My lesson in personhood is that we cannot turn on ourselves when the world is already turning on us.

My students' refusal to be silenced calls me into the space they are taking up — with their flags and dance parties and "that's pretty gay" choruses over everything they love. I won't show my students that fear has constricted my throat any longer, or that an agreement on letterhead can erase my humanity, or that so many averted eyes can keep me from continuing to look out with a smile. I want to risk as much as they are, in asserting our existence without waiting for permission, in speaking freely without waiting to be invited. I want to show my students what it means to be unapologetically trans.

Our humanity as educators is the power that those who seek to privatize and disinvest in public education don't want us to know that we have. We have the power that cannot be regulated by contracts or closed-door agreements or legislation designed to erase humans and history from our classrooms. A teacher in their full humanity and power can recognize the same in their students, and demand better from the education system that dehumanizes all of us. ●

Ty Marshall (he/they) is an 8th-year teacher, currently teaching social studies at McDaniel High School and English language development with Portland DART Schools.

ON BEHALF OF THEIR NAME

USING THEY/THEM PRONOUNS BECAUSE THEY NEED US TO

BY MYKHIEL DEYCH

"When someone with the authority of a teacher describes the world and you are not in it, there is a moment of psychic disequilibrium, as if you looked into a mirror and saw nothing."
—Adrienne Rich

Adrienne Rich's quote illuminated the projector screen welcoming teachers as they entered the library for a 90-minute training on gender and sexuality acceptance led by the Queer-Straight Alliance (QSA) — a student organization that I am the staff advisor for. Our large urban school holds about 100 staff members. Maybe 3 percent looked forward to this training. The rest sat with their arms crossed, present only because the administration mandated their attendance.

The QSA youth pushed for this training all year. At last, late February, here we were. In my final year of probationary teaching, I stood mere weeks away from

receiving my permanent contract. Job security slinked at the brink of my reach. And I feared ruining it all.

I felt panic at the thought of losing my job for being a transgender and queer teacher leading transgender and queer students. This "liberal" community and its wealthy, demanding parents held power and sway that made my nerves pulse irregularly. I woke some nights in a sweat from nightmares of tantrum-throwing parents and their hate-inspired monologues directed at me: "What even are you?! Despicable! Unfit to be around kids — how dare you. Stay away from my kid!" When you are a member of a marginalized group — especially one that's been villainized and degraded — safety is not an automatic privilege, even when you're white. Although my whiteness does provide shelter that trans and queer teachers of color are not afforded.

The students and I met to plan the staff training for several weeks before the February meeting. Youth were both gung-ho and noncommittal. The students wanted to yell at the staff, misgender, and ridicule them. These students hurt and wanted to lash out to ease some of their pain. Many of them felt strongly, but few of them wanted to stay after school for two hours and say anything into the sea of mostly heterosexual, entirely cisgender teachers. They were great balls of fury and they wanted to pitch fire in every direction at once. Few had the energy necessary to face the staff in a meeting.

These teachers were supposed to be theirs. Students say "My teacher." This simple possessive pronoun makes the pain of not being seen by that same teacher feel like a self-inflicted wound. Some teachers ridiculed students in front of the class, scoffing at the idea or trouble of using they/them pronouns. One teacher told our VP: "Well, what is the kid biologically? That's what they are to me." The incredulousness of this statement essentially translates to "What's that kid's genitalia — students are equivalent to their genitalia." No teacher needs to be thinking about children's genitalia.

During the weeks of planning for this training, I floundered in a borderland where I wanted/needed to be with the youth — have their backs and support their lived experiences, listen to them, validate them. But also being an adult and a colleague, I worried that yelling at staff wouldn't change anything. And we needed staff-wide change. Students skipped classes, students hurt — each other and themselves — students avoided their education because adults couldn't just get their names right. Everything begins with a name. We exist because we know each other by name. Youth change their names because this gives them the power to exist. To refuse to call a student by their painstakingly chosen name — whether it matches the gradebook or not — denies a student's right to be wholly present. This erasure snatches away identity just barely emerging.

I kept asking the QSA these questions: "What outcome do you want? What is your purpose in this training? Do you want to educate the teachers? Share your stories so they're known?"

Aliya said, "We want to be seen. We want them to try." Sal added, "How is it so hard to use my right pronoun? Why?"

While politicians and professionals and teachers argue about the morality of gender variance, real children are disappearing in the classroom — figuratively and literally. Two trans students dropped out by second semester, another was on the verge; QSA members barely hung on, and our school later lost a transgender student to suicide. And this in a liberal district at a high school with gender-neutral bathrooms.

I let them hash out their ideas for a couple meetings without much of my own input. I would nod and say yes and affirm. I'd empathize and I meant it all, but inside I was kind of freaking out. Will this implode? Is staff just going to scoff and roll their eyes? Will they even listen or just be on their phones the whole time? What if students don't show? What if my colleagues blame and hate me for this? What if I get fired? Am I really going to come out to my whole staff in this training?

Yes, I am.

As soon as the staff settles into their seats we start off with a video of Olive, the vice president of the QSA. Olive nods at me with tightened lips, and I hit play: "My name is Olive Reed and I use they/them pronouns." The video follows Olive moving through their day and discussing their experiences with school being safer than home but that they are called a faggot nearly every day. Olive says, "Everything in our society is binary, it's not just gender. But when you don't fit into that binary, take a step back and you're like, but what about me? And it's just — it feels like — there's not a place for me in this society." Teachers watch, rapt with attention. Olive believes that "no one should have to hide who they are because of fear. No one should have to be afraid of being able to be who they are."

When I first saw this video, I knew I couldn't support the students in this training and not come out to my colleagues. I owed them the overcoming of my own fear, I owed them my vulnerability. Olive's video ends with a quiet call to action: "People are accepting enough that you can come out, that you can openly be who you are, but people are not accepting enough for everyone to be safe. Yeah, we've made a hell of a lot of progress, but no, we're not anywhere near resolving anything."

At the video's end I instruct staff to write down striking thoughts and questions before sharing out at their tables. Many of the responses reveal appreciation for Olive's bravery and vulnerability. To not overcook Olive's anxiety about being the center of attention we move on to our intros. Three (of several) students and I give our names and pronouns:

"My name is D'Angel, I use he/him pronouns."
"My name is Olive, I use they/them pronouns."
"My name is Asuna, I use she/her pronouns."
My heart pounding against my vocal cords, I finish us off: "My name is Mykhiel Deych, I use they/them pronouns." Shuffle, shuffle. Swallow.

A pulse of invisible energy ripples through the four of us and out over the crowd. Air shimmering like the waving heat over an open grill in summer. D'Angel says with a smile, "Now please go around at your tables and say your names and pronouns." Some eyes roll and lips snarl, yet most of the staff conform to the simple task. A QSA member is seated at nearly every group table to help with intros. I mean, it is simple, isn't it? Just state your name and pronoun. Not far from the common instruction to state your name and birthdate or name and subject you teach. The norm of introductions at the start of a meeting feels familiar. Why the resistance to pronouns?

The prefix "pro" means on behalf of. In English, we have gendered pronouns, so to use a pronoun in place of a person's name imbues onto the person a slew of gendered meaning that acts to define and/or limit the identity of that person. Students struggle to come into their identities no matter what. Becoming a self challenges everyone. One's gender should be a given, right? The easy part, the part of identity you've had since you were a kid, right?

Along with a handout, the next video, *Sex & Gender Identity: An Intro*, briefly defines and explains key terms: Sex is the biological classification of being female or male or intersex and is assigned at birth. Gender Identity is one's deeply held sense about gender and is not the same as sex. Gender Expression is the external manifestations of gender expressed through a variety of ways, including but not limited to clothes, hair, name, pronoun, voice, behavior, etc. Transgender is an umbrella term for people whose gender identity and gender expression differ from their sex. Cisgender is a term for people whose sex at birth matches their gender identity and gender expression. Genderqueer is a term for people who do not identify as part of the female/male binary and may experience themselves as both or neither. Gender-fluid is a term for a gender identity that varies over time. And lastly, the verb that brought us into the room: Misgender. To misgender someone is to identify a person with a gender that they aren't. For example, when you call me a lady or ma'am you have misgendered me.

Teachers start sharing out about any newfound understandings or questions on the video. One teacher shares a painful incident. Mr. Xon says, "I don't know about these things but what I know is that I let a student go to the bathroom and they take a very long time and when they return, I ask them where they've been and the student says, 'I had to go to the gender-neutral bathroom.' OK, but I don't know if that's really what's happened or not." He stays standing for a moment palms open, facing up. He is trying to understand.

The room hushes; I take a slow breath, and another. But before I say anything, Asuna steps forward to respond. "The only gender-neutral bathroom is far from your classroom, and there is almost always a line for it. This is really hard for us. We need you to believe us." This raw bravery and unapologetic vulnerability inspires me and I shiver. Are teachers that most need to hear this absorbing anything? All the students' hard work — is this going to change anything?

To provide a few tangible tools we put up a slide that has problematic phrasing replaced with simple solutions. Sally reads off, "Instead of calling the class to attention with 'ladies and gentlemen' try 'scholars' or 'mathematicians.' Instead of dividing by 'boys and girls' use 'favorite foods' or 'wearing blue,' etc. Avoid blanket statements like 'all boys this' or 'all girls that.'"

A teacher shares out apologetically, "I don't use the they/them pronouns because I just know I'll mess it up." Griffin replies, "Messing up isn't the problem, we know it's hard to get used to, we actually just want you to try." They don't say it with a smile, but it comes out calm. An audible and affirmative "hmm" sounds out at a few of the tables. After sitting for a long time we shake things up.

Kaitlin instructs into the mic: "Please stand up and if you are a dog person stand over here and if you are a cat person please stand over there." She points to the far ends of the room and a gap in the middle widens as teachers move to where they belong. A few students and teachers vacillate between the two sides and end up in the middle with furrowed brows and heads tipped to one side. One teacher raises her hand and says, "Well, I don't like either." Another says, "I used to like dogs but now I'm more about cats, where should I go?" And another asks with a deep shrug, "But I like both. Where do I belong?"

Where do I belong? The question hangs in the air as several teachers release audible gasps as they catch on to the metaphor they've just played out. "Wait, I get it, students maybe feel like this about their gender," Ms. Smith says and taps a finger to her lips. "Or sexuality too, right?" Some eyebrows furrow. Some grins appear. Nods slowly bob through the clumps of solidly "dog people" and solidly "cat people." If only gender was a simple choice.

Teachers chat it out as they return to their seats to try role plays where they practice four important interactions: asking for someone's pronouns, using they/them pronouns in a conversation, correcting someone misgendering someone else, and correcting themselves misgendering someone. I circulate around the tables. At least one student sits amongst each of the table groups. The role plays open a flurry of activity at each table. The air is full of electricity, my breathing feels steady until suddenly, one table gets superheated. I rush over to intervene and arrive in time to hear Kaitlin nearly shout "It is grammatically correct, we already use they/them pronouns when referring to one person when we don't know a person's gender." I lock eyes with Kaitlin and she grins. "I got this M. Deych. Thanks, though." She is proud of herself. Proud to debate a teacher we already knew going into this training would be a wall to take down brick by brick.

When we come back together as a whole group, another teacher asks, "Are we really expected to keep track of when it is and isn't OK to use a student's preferred name or pronoun?" After so much of the training going well, the hostility in this question stuns me speechless. My head races. You know how we have all that training about getting to know students, building relationships?! Well, this is that! To my appreciative surprise, another teacher responds, "Well, we're not talking about a huge percentage of your class here. This comes down to a few students on your whole roster probably." Thank you, allies, I need your help — students need you.

The training finishes with a panel that responds to teachers' anonymous questions written on scraps of paper that were at each table throughout the training. Three students, a parent of a transgender student, and I sit on the panel. Unfortunately, the final question deflates a lot of the gains we'd made: "I just can't use they/them pronouns, it's wrong, and I just can't. What do I do?" I probably don't hide the irritation when I reply. "No one is expecting the grammar to change. It isn't wrong. You use it grammatically, not 'they is home sick' but 'they are home sick.' And if it helps to know, the reason many of us — the reason I — use they/them pronouns is because it reflects the multiplicity that I experience in my gender. So it is actually very right."

Griffin relays their story of battling depression and ends with their head held high. "We actually just need you to try."

The students left feeling hurt by this last statement/question. It haunted them. And though issues persist with certain teachers, overall progress accumulates. Multiple teachers thanked me for supporting the students in that training. One said she felt defensive at first but then it really was good to hear about the students' experiences. Another came to me to hash out and discuss the issue with "ladies and gentlemen."

It's ongoing, the work of showing up for students how they need us to show up.

With about 40 percent of transgender people attempting suicide compared to less than 1 percent of the general population we have to because they actually need us to. ●

Mykhiel Deych has taught language arts at the same school in the same town for the same 10 years that so many big huge things have happened in. They live with their family.

BOREALIS

TEACHING THEM INTO EXISTENCE

BY MYKHIEL DEYCH

Words don't have a tangible weight, so how the hell do they hang so incredibly heavy on the body — stick to me like thistle burrs to wool socks?

A thin, penetrable coat of paint isn't enough to cover the tremor of fear in any body when words have sunk into you — glare at you from the bathroom wall: "The faggots who use this bathroom are gonna be shot."

Maybe if it wasn't the gender-neutral bathroom it wouldn't frighten us so.

Maybe if it wasn't an era of school shootings it wouldn't feel like a direct threat.

Maybe if I wasn't an out trans teacher tending to the tender hearts of the Queer-Straight Alliance (QSA) youth, maybe then I too could turn my other cheek.

The graffiti showed up in the bathroom next to the photography class — the class where Lilith thrived and felt the most herself, the most safe. The only class she never skipped or missed. This was Lilith's bathroom. The one she used when she was still alive.

Suicide is, of course, complex. The final act in a seemingly endless struggle. When the world daily erases you or ingrains in you the notion that you are not worthy — how does one find the strength to face each day? I can't help but wonder if this horrific graffiti was cut No. 1,001.

Lilith chose to be a senior mentor for my 9th-grade English class before we had ever met or knew each other. Most students are mentors for teachers who they had when they were 9th graders, but Lilith chose me because I'm the only trans teacher in the school and she is an openly trans girl. She was.

Lilith was seeking something in me: connection maybe, acknowledgement, comfort, safety perhaps. I don't know, because whatever it was, she didn't get it from me. I tried to connect, but minimally so. We chatted and she revealed how much she writes and I said I'd love to read her writing; she never brought it in and I never asked again. She started regularly skipping classes and I'd send notes about missing her on the progress reports but I didn't call home — why didn't I call home? I mean, she was a senior mentor, not really my student, not really a role that most students take too seriously, not really — why didn't I reach her? Why didn't I do more?

Rationally, her suicide is not my fault, I'm a blip in the grand story of her life, but emotionally, she was within reach and I failed to clutch. I failed Lilith.

Teaching isn't supposed to include life-or-death consequences, but it does. When it comes to LGBTQ students, we fail to hold space for their existence. Heterocentric, cisnormative curriculum writes out the existence of LGBTQ lives. Campaigns such as Dan Savage's "It Gets Better" spur and go viral precisely because we aren't actually reassuring youth that their existence is acceptable, real, normal. We need an "It Gets Better" campaign because high school is awful for LGBTQ kids, high school is fatal.

Teaching isn't supposed to include life-or-death consequences, but it does.

How many LGBTQ authors do you teach about? How often is the intersection and difference of sexuality and gender addressed in your Socratic seminars? Do you discuss transgender history in U.S. history? Do you reveal authors' struggles with sexuality and how these relate to their art? Has gay culture ever been given the credit it deserves for spurring numerous fashion, music, and art trends? No, and me neither. As an out trans and gay teacher I can't always fend off the fear of a parental uprising about my "gay agenda." This sort of bravery hasn't yet materialized in my classroom, but I'm working on it.

Please, don't leave it for the out gay and trans teachers to do this work. Please, I'm begging you to use your heterosexual cisnormative privilege for good. Teach LGBTQ lives into existence. ●

Mykhiel Deych has taught language arts at the same school in the same town for the same 10 years that so many big huge things have happened in. They live with their family.

HOW WE FAILED NIGEL SHELBY AND ALLOWED THE ABUSE HE ENDURED

BY MAXIMILLIAN MATTHEWS

There was Marsha P. Johnson, Sylvia Rivera, Audre Lorde, Barbara Smith, bell hooks, RuPaul, James Earl Hardy, E. Lynn Harris, Essex Hemphill, Bayard Rustin, and of course, James Baldwin. I did not know about any of them when I needed them most. I could not find *In the Life, This Bridge Called My Back, Black Feminist Thought,* or *Paris Is Burning* in my school's library. Authority figures who did not even know me were choosing the materials I had access to. Although I attended the Blackest high school, Hillside High, in my liberal hometown of Durham, North Carolina, I still did not see the examples of queerness I needed as a teenager.

My friends and I joke about having gaydar, an innate awareness of when another queer person is in our presence. Those brief moments when you make eye contact with "fam" as we like to call them or the instances when you observe the way somebody walks is what usually makes our gaydar ring the alarm. I longed to hear that alarm when I walked the hallways of Hillside. I longed to read about someone who was attracted to men like I was. I longed to see someone who rejected the labels assigned to them as I struggled to do. There was a time when all I wanted was a confirmation I was not alone in my queerness.

Despite the few examples that existed as I grew up in the '90s, the isolation I felt led me to consider suicide. In my mind, death was better than loneliness. Tragically, I was already battling a system that determined conservatism was better than queerness, normalcy better than diversity, conformity better than nonconformity, and whiteness better than Blackness. This was the system that decided what I did and did not see, what received approval and what did not, and whose life had value and whose did not. It was a system constructed to intentionally exclude, oppress, marginalize, and eradicate people like me and Nigel Shelby.

After enduring antagonism and bullying from his peers, Nigel Shelby of Huntsville, Alabama, died by suicide at the age of 15. Nigel was a 9th grader at Huntsville High School. As the news spread, I saw tributes and condolences on my social media timelines. On April 20, GLSEN Greater Huntsville wrote "Nigel, we will always remember you. You're gone too soon and tonight our hearts are heavy" on their Facebook page. Writer George M. Johnson tweeted "Queer kids are dying while we wait on folk to grow out of homophobia. . . . Homophobia has Black children committing suicide. . . . It costs you NOTHING to love a queer child."

Black children dying by suicide is nothing new. Considering the depth, magnitude, and predominance of anti-Blackness, there will be Black children who choose suicide. The intent of anti-Blackness is to inflict harm on Black lives and keep Blackness subjugated. The same applies to homophobia and its impact on gay lives. As we see with Nigel and other Black children before him, bullying is an effective way to perform the work of anti-Blackness and homophobia. To endure both can simply be far too burdensome for a child. Even in this age where Pride celebrations have become mainstreamed and Black queer folks are visible across genres, it is still not enough to eliminate the realities of intersectional oppression.

In the Human Rights Campaign's 2019 *Black & African American LGBTQ Youth Report*, the following data were reported:

- 80 percent of Black LGBTQ youth "usually" feel depressed or down.
- 71 percent "usually" feel worthless or hopeless.
- 40 percent have been bullied on school property within the last 12 months.
- 67 percent have been verbally insulted because of their LGBTQ identity.
- 30 percent have been physically threatened because of their LGBTQ identity.
- 35 percent received counseling in the past year.
- 35 percent can "definitely" be themselves in school.

Nigel was particularly vulnerable to these realities in Alabama. Advocates for

Youth reports LGBTQ youth in Alabama are marginalized and at risk for negative health outcomes. "The national Youth Risk Behavior Survey found that 11 percent to 30 percent of gay and lesbian students and 12 percent to 25 percent of bisexual students surveyed did not go to school at least one day during the prior month because of safety concerns. These concerns put LGBTQ youth [in Alabama] at greater risk for depression, substance use, and sexual behaviors that place them at risk for HIV and STIs (Advocates for Youth, 2016)." Under Alabama law, schools that offer sex education must emphasize homosexuality "is not a lifestyle acceptable to the general public" and that "homosexual conduct is a criminal offense under the laws of the state (Ala.Code 16-40A2-2(a)(8)." To further illustrate the climate Alabama Black LGBTQ youth live in, an Alabama police officer was placed on leave after making anti-LGBTQ comments on a Facebook post about Nigel's death.

We know that Nigel was "the sweetest child," "outgoing," "always full of joy, full of light," and suffered from bouts of depression, according to his mother. We also know he was open about his sexuality. This placed him at greater risk for experiencing harassment and abuse. Although there is a popular refrain in society that "It gets better" for LGBTQ youth, this could not be further from the truth for some, particularly for Black LGBTQ youth. When we say "It gets better," we ignore how impactful the present can be. The U.S. Department of Health and Human Services states that children who are bullied are more likely to experience depression, anxiety, and decreased academic achievement. By underestimating the effects these can have on a child's mental health and not addressing this country's bullying crisis with urgency, we fail the children who need us the most, as Nigel did.

When we say "It gets better," we ignore how impactful the present can be.

I told my mother about my suicidal ideations when I was a high school freshman. She heeded the alerts I displayed, removed me from the honors level courses I was taking, and connected me with my high school's band director who placed me in the marching band. He mentored me and took an interest in my life that inspired me to keep going. Gioncarlo Valentine writes, "We need to pay attention to the signs and the intricacies of what the children in our lives are going through, prioritizing it in a way that is nothing short of intentional." The intention and swiftness with which my mother responded to my cries is rare; it is how we all must approach the needs of Black LGBTQ youth. I cannot help but wonder if Nigel cried out as I did.

Did he write about his struggles in an English assignment? Did he look distressed or on the verge of tears as he tried to concentrate in class? Did his teachers mark him tardy because he had to take the long way to class to avoid his bullies? Did he eat his lunch in the bathroom so he wouldn't have to go in the cafeteria and be seen? Did he have any safe spaces at his school? Besides his mother who was clearly invested in his life, did the other adults in his life simply ask Nigel how he was doing or if he needed anything? We have the opportunity to do those things now.

Although it won't bring back Nigel, Giovanni, Blake, Ashawnty, Gabriel, Carl, and the other Black children who have died due to suicide, you can observe the Black LGBTQ children in your life more closely. You can learn more about the mental health resources available to them in your local community. You can create them if you feel there aren't enough. You can empower and educate Black LGBTQ children. You can advocate for bullying prevention programs, laws, policies, regulations, and protections for LGBTQ youth. You can volunteer and partner with local LGBTQ organizations. You can hold your local elected officials and school districts accountable for the decisions they make. You can organize for Black LGBTQ youth. The most effective of them all, you can speak to Black LGBTQ youth directly.

In times like these, we can easily get discouraged and wonder if the work is in vain. For the sake of the Black LGBTQ youth still with us, resist.

In times like these, we can easily get discouraged and wonder if the work is in vain. For the sake of the Black LGBTQ youth still with us, resist. ●

Maximillian Matthews (all gender pronouns respectfully) is a Black nonbinary queer writer based out of Durham, North Carolina. Maximillian's work has also been featured on Black Youth Project, Afropunk, and The Body Is Not an Apology. Maximillian has worked in higher education administration for more than 10 years. They are currently pursuing a master's in mental health counseling at North Carolina Agricultural and Technical State University. Their self-published collection of essays titled Another World *has been praised as "a thoughtful and necessary book" by Kirkus Reviews.*

RESOURCES

Advocates for Youth. 2016. *Young People in Alabama.* Retrieved from www.advocatesforyouth.org/wp-content/uploads/storage//advfy/documents/Young-People-in-Alabama.pdf

Centers for Disease Control and Prevention. 2017. *Youth Risk Behavior Surveillance — United States, 2017.* Retrieved from www.cdc.gov/mmwr/volumes/67/ss/pdfs/ss6708a1-h.pdf

This article was first published on Black Youth Project.

CAN A 4-YEAR-OLD KNOW HER GENDER IDENTITY? YES.

THE IMPORTANCE OF SUPPORTING GENDER-EXPANSIVE STUDENTS

BY ESPERANZA ANDERSON

Warm and cozy, lying in bed, his head rested on my shoulder. My son's pudgy little 4-year-old arm was wrapped around my chest as I read the picture book *Jacob's New Dress* at his request for the umpteenth time over the past week:

"'There are lots of ways to be a boy,' Jacob's mom said."

I paused and looked at my son.

"Do you believe that, Simon?"

I paused again and did not get a reply.

I tried rephrasing my question: "How is school going? Do kids say anything about the dresses you wear?"

He took a deep breath and replied "No."

Sensing something was weighing on him I followed up: "Do you believe that there are lots of ways to be a boy? That boys can wear dresses?"

He finally replied. "Yeah," and I followed up with "Do you feel like a boy?"

"No, mom. I'm a girl."

My daughter's statement could not have been more direct, honest, and clear. In that moment I glimpsed how deeply gender-expansive people feel who they are, no matter what society has labeled them as at birth.

All schools have gender-expansive students, whether they are "out" or not, affirmed or chastised. In Pittsburgh, researchers found that nearly one in 10 students in more than a dozen public high schools identified as gender-expansive. That is five times the current national estimates. In my 10 years as an elementary school teacher, I have had four gender-expansive students who I know of, and there are currently nine gender-expansive students who are "out" in our elementary school of 250 kids.

COLIN LAUREL

Often on people's minds is a huge question, as it was on my mind when my 4-year-old was adamant about being a girl: Can a child this young actually know if they identify differently from their assigned gender at birth?

Yes.

This is not to say I have always felt this way. I have questioned, pushed back, and dealt with grief and anger when processing my own child's gender identity. What I have come to understand is how a person identifies is not about others' perception, it is about how they are authentically themselves. I have done research, met with a gender clinic counselor at Kaiser Permanente, taken a class on the gender spectrum at Lewis & Clark College in Portland, and with all my being believe the answer to that question is yes. Young children absolutely know inside how they experience gender. They may need help finding the words to express themselves, and people who will truly listen, see, and support their authenticity, but 100 percent young kids know.

The American Academy of Pediatrics outlines the stages of gender identity development and by age 4 most children have a stable sense of their gender identity: "The point is that all children tend to develop a clearer view of themselves and their gender over time. At any point, research suggests that children who assert a gender-diverse identity know their gender as clearly and consistently as their developmentally matched peers and benefit from the same level of support, love, and social acceptance."

Before my own child came out, I was supportive of gender-expansive children in my classroom, trying to do my best to affirm their gender. I changed gendered teaching practices like using boy/girl circles as a quick and easy way to mix up seating patterns. (This practice is not only gender non-inclusive but sexist, assuming that if students of the same gender don't sit next to each other they won't talk as much.) I also advocated for gender-expansive students by helping other teachers use correct pronouns and think about classroom routines and practices that are not inclusive. However, until the journey with my own child, I did not fully understand the depths of the pain people experience when not affirmed, nor the tremendous joy when they are.

A 2022 study by the Human Rights Campaign and the University of Connecticut found:

- over half of transgender and gender-expansive youth surveyed "reported feeling unsafe in at least one school setting."
- less than 1 in 6 transgender and gender-expansive youth surveyed "are always referred to by the correct pronouns at school."

In the week following my daughter vocalizing who she is, I asked her if it was important for others to know. On the way to school one morning, she told me to tell her teachers. So, upon entering the classroom filled with little people playing with blocks, pouring sand, dressing up, and shrieks of disagreement and bubbles of laughter, I did. The teacher thanked us for sharing and asked what pronouns to use.

I was thrown. I didn't know how to answer.

As a teacher this would have been my question too, but as a parent I wasn't yet able to process the immense mental shift needed to fully see and affirm my child. Having this simple question reflected back at me made it real. I knew that I had to take my daughter's authenticity seriously.

The majority of resources use the guidelines that when a child is *consistent, insistent,* and *persistent,* they are gender-expansive. It is important to note that gender identity is different from gender expression. Gender identity is how a person experiences their gender — how they feel inside. Gender expression is a person's behavior, mannerisms, and appearance that are usually associated with societal expectations of femininity and masculinity. Before my daughter came out, I thought she was experimenting with gender expression. For nearly six months before announcing she is a girl, she had asked to grow out her hair and would only wear dresses.

With the direct and clear message my child was giving, in addition to the months of shifting gender expression, within the week after that October night when she looked me in the eye and said "I am a girl," and with lots of reading and discussions with her father, she transitioned socially. We started using female pronouns.

Then there was the issue of her name: Simon.

After school one day, kids burst out of the classroom, running into their caregivers' arms, dropping coats, lugging backpacks half their size. A grandmother next to me said "What's your daughter's name?" As my daughter walked up with her hot pink space-themed tulle dress, I said "Simon."

"Nice to meet you, Simona!" she replied.

The rest of the conversation is a blur. All I could think about was how I didn't correct the grandmother. My heart ached as I knew I had not protected my daughter. I let my own desire to not make someone else uncomfortable, along with a mixture of my own uncertainty, get in the way of supporting this brave child.

This experience forced me to grapple with my own fears and also how important it is for young gender-expansive people to be taught explicitly about the language used to describe who they are and how society is set up to fit people into a binary. For example, just how gendered names are.

On the walk home we talked.

I mostly talked:

"How was the day?

"Did you get the dinosaurs out during outdoor play?"

"What songs did you sing?"

She was not very talkative.

Then I stopped. I had to apologize.

I knelt down so I could be eye to eye with my daughter.

"I should have corrected that grandma when she called you Simona. I am sorry."

She was quiet and stared at the sidewalk.

"I think she called you Simona because it sounds like Simon and it's a girl's name."

At this point, I knew we had to talk about how names are gendered.

"Dad and I named you Simon when you were born because we thought you were a boy. We were wrong. You absolutely can keep that name and if people get confused I will do better to correct them. You can also choose a new name to try out. A girl's name."

At this her eyes lit up and she smiled.

She wasn't sure what to choose so I asked if she wanted help. I shared that we would have named her Simone if we'd known she was a girl.

Simone it is.

On that crisp fall day, on the sidewalk by 7-Eleven, Simone was affirmed.

The journey we are on has lots of joy but also pain.

The world we live in is not safe for gender-expansive people. The Human Rights Campaign reported "the deaths of at least 30 transgender and gender non-conforming people whose lives have been tragically and inhumanely taken through violent means, including through gun and interpersonal violence, in 2023." Of these, 87 percent were people of color, including 50 percent who were Black transgender women. This number does not account for those attacked or brutally beaten who survived.

Not just the physical threats but the emotional pain gender-expansive people often feel is immense, and the risk of suicide or self-harm is high if people are not affirmed. Simone made comments before feeling affirmed about not liking her body that speak volumes to how much pain people feel when their gender identity does not match what society has deemed acceptable for the gender they are.

I continued to support Simone with the language she needed to understand the gender spectrum.

Wanting my child to feel gender congruence, the feeling of harmony with one's gender, I did as much research as I could, including joining a parent support group, and I continued to support Simone with the language she needed to understand the gender spectrum. There are children's books that break down the gender binary for ways to talk about bodies and gender identity. Thankfully, in addition to the resources I've used, and as more people in her life affirmed and understood who she is, now at age 7 she has stopped saying negative things about her body or wanting to harm it. What has also been shown through research is that gender-expansive youth who report having at least one gender-affirming space were 25 percent less likely to attempt suicide in the past year.

As teachers, we can create gender-affirming school spaces by honoring students' pronouns and helping all students and families understand the gender spectrum. There is a wide range of picture books that have characters who are gender-expansive, ranging from gender expression that does not match the binary to transgender kids going through a social transition.

In addition to helping all students understand the wide range of how people experience gender, we can make sure gender-expansive children have a bathroom they are comfortable using at school. Advocating and establishing gender-inclusive restrooms is ideal but if a school's leadership is not responsive to this, the next best bathroom option is to make sure they have access to a single-user restroom (usually those designated for adults/teachers). There are also resources that provide checklists for gender-expansive students and can be used by teachers and parents.

One of the most transformative ways we can support gender-expansive students is to keep learning. Most of us have grown up in a traditional setting that is overwhelmingly binary; our mindsets need to expand. Terminology is also shifting as communities change and gender-expansive people share more about their experiences.

My advice: Be willing to grow, change, and make mistakes. Own our mistakes and keep growing. I will never fully grasp my child's experience or those of my gender-expansive students. The marginalization they face in an overwhelmingly binary world is intense. I am inspired by gender-expansive people authentically showing up in a world that tries to erase their existence.

As a cisgender woman I don't know what it feels like to fight for my existence. However, I do know the importance of believing gender-expansive people and supporting them. Gender-expansive people are strong and their existence and willingness to let others know who they are is a revolutionary act. As teachers and parents, especially those of us who are cisgender, we can use our privilege to make the world a more inclusive and safer place.

We must face the fact that our school systems systemically damage gender-expansive people — people who do not fit in the nice little box of blue and pink, boy or girl.

Even though we live in a world that overwhelmingly does not affirm and actively tries to oppress and harm gender-expansive people, those living authentically also experience tremendous joy. As teachers we can be co-conspirators and advocates for creating spaces that will allow our gender-expansive students to thrive just like we hope for all our students. ●

Esperanza Anderson (she/her) has been an elementary school teacher for the past 16 years. She currently works as an instructional coach supporting teachers with culturally relevant strategies, and as an adjunct teacher for MAT graduate students. She asked to be identified by a pseudonym for this article, and has used a pseudonym for her daughter.

CHAPTER TWO

TEACHING TRANS CURRICULUM

NO PRIDE for SOME of US without
LIBERATION for ALL OF US
MARSHA "Pay It No Mind" JOHNSON
was a mother of the trans + queer liberation movement. She dedicated her life to helping trans youth, sex workers and poor and incarcerated queers.
We HONOR her LEGACY by Supporting TRANS WOMEN of COLOR to
LIVE + LEAD.
MICAH BAZANT

QUEERING BLACK HISTORY AND GETTING FREE

BY DOMINIQUE HAZZARD

I am a queer Black woman. By this I mean that my sexuality exists outside the margins, between the approved boundaries, beyond the limits of most imaginations. A queer thing is a thing that existing words cannot yet adequately describe, a thing that our language and our boxes have not yet evolved to capture. So, what does queering something mean? To me it means turning the thing on its head: questioning its assumed narratives, reworking its categories, and upending its status quo.

Let's queer Black history.

LIFTING UP THE STORIES OF BLACK LGBTQ PEOPLE

Queering Black history means lifting up the stories of Black LGBTQ people. It means resolving that not one more student learns about the "I Have a Dream" speech without learning about Bayard Rustin, the man who led the planning of the March on Washington for Jobs and Freedom — at least not on our watch. It means really learning about him: knowing his contributions to the Civil Rights Movement, reading *Time on Two Crosses* right next to *The Autobiography of Martin Luther King Jr.*, having discussions in our classrooms and on our social media about "Letter from a Birmingham Jail" while also discussing why Bayard Rustin too was arrested, how he was relegated to the background by his peers, and what we must do to prevent that from ever again happening in the Black freedom movement.

Queering Black history means canonizing Marsha P. Johnson as a matriarch of Black America. Putting her face on those calendars and poster collages right next to Harriet Tubman, Sojourner Truth, Coretta Scott King, and Michelle Obama. It means studying her ACT UP campaigns in high school classrooms. It means mourning her too-early death just as we mourn the deaths of cisgender men like Malcolm and Medgar. It means examining why it took 20 years for the NYPD to investigate that death as a murder, and having conversations about the role of the Black freedom movement in bringing about trans liberation today.

COMPLICATING THE STORIES OF THE HISTORICAL FIGURES WE KNOW

Queering Black history goes wider and deeper than the inclusion and re-centering of queer folks. Remember that queering also means reworking. We must rework and complicate the stories we tell about the Black figures we are familiar with.

Rosa Parks, for example, was not only told to get to the back of the bus. She was also told by Montgomery NAACP president E. D. Nixon, with whom she served as chapter secretary, that women should stay in the kitchen. As we study her resistance against both attacks on her Black womanhood (and her organizing against sexual violence), a queering of Black history requires us to ask why we leave out that piece of the story, and how we can ensure that our contemporary movements are safe spaces for people living at the intersections.

Billie Holiday was a prolific jazz singer. She was also addicted to heroin, and the first major target of the federal government's war on drugs. Harry Anslinger, virulent racist and first head of the Federal Bureau of Narcotics, intentionally turned a blind eye to the addictions of prominent white entertainers while obsessing over Holiday and his dream of bringing the full force of the federal government down upon her head. She died shackled to a hospital bed, denied appropriate treatment by the federal government, with police officers at her door. Billie Holiday has an important place not only in the history of Black music, but also in the history of Black people, the police state, and resistance.

Remember that queering also means reworking.

SEEKING OUT NEW STORIES

But if we are to queer Black history then we must dig deeper, do more than adding nuance to the narratives of those we already know and love. We also have to study and celebrate the Black people who have been erased, hidden from our collective memories. We have to move beyond the shiny Negroes — the astronauts, entrepreneurs, athletes, entertainers, and organizers who have been deemed respectable enough to be worthy of our memory. We have to look between the cracks and find our incarcerated heroes, our undocumented leaders, our luminary sex workers, the people who systems of oppression most desperately want us to forget. And we have to teach those stories to each other.

We have to do the work of intentionally remembering people like Carol Crooks. I learned her name while doing research for this essay. She doesn't have a Wikipedia page. But she is worth remembering. Crooks was a woman who became an organizer while incarcerated at Bedford Hills, a maximum security prison in New York.

In February of 1974, Crooks had a severe migraine and asked to be taken to see the prison nurse. When her guard denied her request, she tried to push past her and get to the nurse anyway. In response to this incident, Crooks was beaten, stripped naked, and placed into a solitary confinement cell for three days. Crooks later filed a lawsuit challenging the practice of sentencing inmates to solitary confinement with no trial or formal charges. She won her case, and the warden was found guilty of unconstitutional treatment of a prisoner.

> **Queering Black history means remembering everyday people.**

That August, Crooks was returned to solitary with no formal charges. The next morning, a group of women went to the warden and demanded Crooks' release, alleging that the solitary confinement of Crooks was retaliatory. The women were ignored and told to go to bed three hours earlier than usual. They refused to comply. The guards began to assault the women in response to the insubordination. The women seized the guards' weapons and fought back. They took over the prison in what is now known as the August Rebellion, until state troopers subdued them about four hours later.

Carol Crooks is part of a queered Black history.

DISRUPTING THE CENTRALIZED, CHARISMATIC LEADER NARRATIVE

Next we must question the very ideal of Black history through the lens of the individual. We must ask ourselves: Why does the history we choose to remember so often come in the form of charismatic and solitary pioneers, centralized leadership, and the folks out front?

Queering Black history means remembering everyday people, the struggles they faced, and the work they did. It means recognizing ordinary Black people who were told their lives didn't matter, but who still contained a fierce will to live, and love, and fight for freedom. It means valuing all different types of Black leadership — the folks who were behind the scenes, who were quiet, who were less than charming, who didn't win but set the stage for those who later would, who rose to the occasion because they had to and then went back to their regularly scheduled lives. It means celebrating collectives, and group efforts, and conglomerations of movers, shakers, and neighbors whose names we won't ever know.

I want us to upend the status quo by including the Contract Buyers League in our Civil Rights Movement narrative. The Contract Buyers League was a group of more than 500 people living on the South Side of Chicago in the 1960s who had bought their homes through predatory loans after being shut out of the mainstream home loan market by racist laws. They banded together, filed suit against the speculators who were cheating them, and demanded their money back. They lost. But the Contract Buyers League is part of a queered Black history.

I want us to queer Black history by teaching about the residents of the Arthur Capper public housing community in Washington, D.C. These residents saw businesses, and particularly grocery stores, disinvest from their Southeast community in the 1970s. They decided to take matters into their own hands. As the mythology of entitled Black welfare queens and lazy project thugs was gaining steam across the country, the residents worked together to start a community-owned small business. They built the Martin Luther King Jr. Co-Op Food Store and harnessed the power of cooperative economics to nourish a Black community trying to survive in a hostile white world. We don't know the names of everyone who accomplished this feat, but the residents of the now-demolished Arthur Capper public housing project are part of a queered Black history.

ACKNOWLEDGING OUR DIRT, HOLDING OUR PAIN

A queered Black history cannot be sanitized. Filing down Black history's sharp edges would make sense if the only point of studying it was to make ourselves feel good. Sweeping the flaws of our Black icons under the rug would be reasonable if the goal of Black history was to convince a white society that Black people are good and smart, that we can be honorable too, that our lives matter. But I don't believe that either of these goals are what Black history is about.

> **A queered Black history cannot be sanitized.**

I believe that we learn Black history because doing so will help us to get free. And in order to accomplish this goal, to be able to learn from the fullness of our past, we have to approach it with a queer lens. We have to bring to Black history a quality that the Black queer community embodies at its best — the unconditional acceptance of people's full and real selves.

Our history is what it is. Sometimes we didn't overcome. Sometimes our faves were misogynists. Sometimes our idols were reckless and led movements into the ground. Sometimes effective and powerful Black leaders were on crack. Sometimes our stories are not glistening tales of hope and triumph and movin' on up, but stories of mistakes made. Sometimes they are stories of pain and loss, death, and things being taken from us. But they are stories that have something to teach us nonetheless.

Let's queer Black history. Let's reimagine it as an opportunity to celebrate Black heroes, leaders, and everyday people. Let's use it to remember and mourn the Black lives that white supremacy has ripped from our arms. Let's use it as a chance to learn from the lives of Black people at all different intersections, Black people whose sweat and tears, laughter and joy, victories and mistakes have brought us to where we are today. Let's make learning Black history about getting free. ●

Dominique Hazzard is a food justice advocate, a Black freedom organizer, and a doctoral student at Johns Hopkins University studying the history of racial capitalism, land use, and the environment. This article originally appeared on Black Youth Project and also appeared in the book Teaching for Black Lives.

EXPANDING INTERSECTIONAL QUEER HISTORY IN THE ELEMENTARY GRADES

BY LAURA SHELTON

EBIIN LEE

My 5th- and 6th-grade students gathered as I drew a tree on chart paper. "This tree represents a person. The branches are all different parts of who this person is. We call these identities. Everyone has many identities that make up who they are." I labeled some of the branches race, gender, language, ethnicity, religion, and left some blank. "What other identities might be listed on our tree?"

"What's ethnicity?" Ashley asked. I saw a sketchbook in her lap and wondered how she had brought it to the carpet without my noticing. She was also drawing and labeling a tree — much more detailed than mine.

"Ethnicity means the country or region where someone is from, or the culture they belong to," I answered. I added the definition to the label. "Over the next few weeks, we will learn about every identity listed here and some that aren't on the tree yet, and we will learn about how these identities affect each other and work together to make us who we are."

I posed my question again: "What other identities might we want to add to our tree?"

Mason raised his hand slowly, then put it down. "Mason, what are you thinking about?" I asked.

"What about people who are gay?" Mason asked quietly.

"You're right, Mason! That is missing from our tree. We call that identity sexual orientation," I answered as some students giggled. "Sexual orientation just means who you like or love. For example, some men love women, and we call that identity heterosexual. The prefix hetero- means different. However, the prefix homo- means the same, and some men are homosexual, meaning they love men. We also call that gay."

Asim raised his hand, "My teacher at my other school told us we weren't allowed to say that word at school." Other students nodded.

I nodded: "Sometimes gay gets used as a put-down, and that's inappropriate, but gay as an identity is valid and we need to talk about it in school so we stop using it as a put-down. We talk about all the identities here because it's important to consider what makes someone who they are as we try to understand history and the world as it is today. Look at this tree," I said as I pointed at my drawing. "If I cover up one of the branches, I will be missing a part of who this person is and how they experience the world."

I taught the identity tree lesson, which was based on Shane Safir's work in her daughter's classroom (see Resources at the end of this article), during the inaugural year of our new grassroots charter school in Greensboro, North Carolina. The school centers restorative justice and allows teachers, students, and community members to co-construct curricula together based on relevant social issues that affect the community and world at large. The school's student population is racially diverse with students coming from several nearby districts, and the school has a significant population of LGBTQ students and families.

I shared the identity tree lesson with my fellow 5th- and 6th-grade co-teachers during planning that same afternoon and one co-teacher suggested participating in GLSEN's Ally Week, now called Solidarity Week (see Resources). We decided our participation in Ally Week would become part of a larger unit in the beginning of the year focused on intersectional identity. As we curated resources for this brief unit, we adapted content from GLSEN and the Human Rights Campaign Welcoming Schools program (see Resources).

The activities outlined in this article are my adaptations of content that our team planned and implemented to help 5th- and 6th-grade students create an intersectional awareness of LGBTQ identities. Due to the limited time within Ally Week and our unit on identity, the goal was to lay a foundation for students to understand the ways that intersectional queerness affects the experiences of LGBTQ individuals. With the current increase of anti-trans legislation and now Florida's Don't Say Gay bill, it's imperative for our students to see examples of LGBTQIA+ people in the past, present, and their future.

INTRODUCING INTERSECTIONALITY

One day after our mid-morning snack break, I wrote the letters LGBTQ on the board, with the letters L, G, B, in green; T in blue; and Q in red. I asked, "Does anyone know what these letters stand for?"

Mason raised his hand. "G is gay," he responded, "and I think L is for les-bee-ann or something like that."

"Lesbian," I corrected, "Yes, and remember that gay is referring to men who love men. What does it mean for someone to be a lesbian?"

Virginia raised her hand. "My aunt is lesbian. She likes women."

I added the words "gay" and "lesbian" underneath the letters. Nora raised her hand and said "B is for bisexual. I know because I am bisexual." She laughed nervously.

"Thank you so much for sharing that with us, Nora," I watched Nora as she heard my words. Her eyes started to tear up.

"Are you OK?" Mason asked.

"Yeah. It's just I haven't told anybody that before, but I like boys and girls," Nora responded, wiping away a tear.

"You must really trust us to tell the class that you are bisexual. Thank you for sharing who you are with us." I walked over to the identity tree and continued: "Friends, remember, someone's sexual orientation is part of who they are, and this is important because it can affect the way they experience the world in the way people treat them. They may get teased or experience discrimination because they are gay, bisexual, or lesbian. If we look only at the tree branch labeled gender or sexual orientation, we aren't seeing the whole person, and we may treat them differently if they are different from what we're used to. However, if we look at someone but completely ignore gender or sexuality, we aren't seeing the full picture of who someone is either, and these are two things that lead to bias and discrimination. We are creating a classroom community in these first weeks of school, and we want everyone to feel safe and welcome here."

I continued the lesson and pointed out that the letters L, G, and B were in green because they were related to sexuality; T was blue because it stood for transgender because people who are transgender identify with a gender other than what they were assigned at birth, and gender really refers to how someone expresses themselves; and Q was in red because queer can refer to gender or sexuality. I left our color-coded letters on the board to refer to throughout Ally Week and the rest of our identity unit. When students would occasionally forget what different letters or words meant, we would refer back to the chart.

In our larger unit on identity, I had started to notice that students were decontextualizing other identities that queer figures had, like their race, socioeconomic status, disability, ethnicity, and language. So I decided we would read the picture book *IntersectionAllies: We Make Room for All.* Kimberlé Crenshaw writes the foreword of the book, and I note she coined the term "intersectionality," which we refer to in other units throughout the year. As we visit and revisit this topic, we come to define intersectionality as the ways overlapping marginalized identities can lead to intersectional oppression and also be a source of solidarity and pride. The book introduces several characters with different identities and describes how each character advocates for their friends whether they share identities or not. The end of the book has overviews of each character and their specific identities. This book helps illustrate the ways that thinking about intersectionality can help build solidarity across groups.

"Do we know for sure that Nia is a girl?"

After I finished reading the book to the class in our meeting space, I closed the cover and pointed to our identity tree. "What did you notice about the characters in the book? Were there any you identified with or were curious to know more about?"

Asim raised his hand. "I noticed Nia and I think she was referring to the Black Lives Matter protests."

I opened to Nia's page. "What identities did Nia have based on the text?"

Asim studied the picture. "She's Black, and a girl, and she's brave because she's standing up to the cops."

"And she has a cat," exclaimed Ashley.

"Where would we put these things on our tree?" I asked.

Nora: "Her gender is girl and her race is Black or African American."

"Do we know for sure that Nia is a girl?" I turned to the Book Notes section of the book. I read aloud "Kimberlé Crenshaw first made up the word intersectionality to describe how the criminal justice system treats Black women and girls like Nia and her mom differently than Black men and white women."

"So, she is a girl," Virginia said.

"Yes, and remember, Nia's identities as a Black girl affect how she experiences the world, and that would be different from a white girl."

Suddenly Nora jumped up. "Wait a second. I'm Black and white. I'm a girl. I'm bisexual. I'm Muslim. Is that what Kimberlé Crenshaw meant?"

"Sort of," I took a beat and searched for words. Nora was picking up on how she holds multiple identities at once but I wasn't quite sure how to answer her question because her understanding of intersectionality was missing how her identities overlapped to create intersecting points of oppression. I knew I needed to explain further, but it didn't seem appropriate to have students reflect on their own levels of oppression at this point.

"I am going to need to think about this more in order to really answer your question, Nora," I responded. "I think it's super important that you are noticing all of these identities that you have. Turn and talk with an elbow partner about some of the identities you share with the characters in the book." I knew that giving students time to reflect on their identities would help them make connections with the book and the other content we had been discussing in our unit on identity as well as Ally Week, but more information would be needed as we continued to unpack queer identities.

QUEER HISTORICAL FIGURES

That evening, I thought a lot about Nora's question. I decided to introduce a diverse group of historical figures during morning meetings for the rest of Ally Week. Students would read a short biography of one person each morning. Then we would relate the text to our identity tree to connect their queerness back to other identities in order to build our understanding of intersectionality. We started with Pauli Murray.

As I called everyone to the meeting space, I pulled out a photo of Pauli Murray and read a summary I had created about them using various websites.

Virginia stopped me mid-sentence. "Why do you keep saying them, he, or she?"

"Pauli Murray had a broader definition of gender. At some points in their life they identified as a woman and used she/her, and at other points Pauli identified as a man and used he/him. Let's think about what Pauli's identity tree may have looked like." I looked over at the chart again. The class sat in silence for a moment, then Mason suddenly cocked his head to one side.

"What did you notice, Mason?" I asked.

"Pauli was Black and Christian, but I don't know about their gender."

I looked back at the summary. "Sometimes the words we use to describe ourselves change over time. We don't know exactly how Pauli described themself, and we know it shifted throughout their life. Now we might call that gender-fluid, nonbinary, or genderqueer. These terms didn't exist when Pauli was alive, but many genderqueer people did. In fact, the word queer itself was considered a huge insult during that time but has since been reclaimed — meaning that LGBTQ people have taken the word that meant something harmful and have adapted it to mean something positive." Even though oppression is an important part of intersectionality, I also wanted to highlight the way identities are sources of pride and solidarity.

At the same time, I think it is important that students understand what intersectional oppression might look like. "We could say simply that Pauli was trans, meaning they have a gender identity different from the sex they were assigned at birth," I continued. "Pauli experienced oppression because they were Black, queer, trans, and assigned female at birth. Even though they were also probably a source of pride and solidarity, Pauli's Blackness meant they were excluded, their queerness meant they were excluded, their transness meant they were excluded, and their femaleness meant they were excluded. For example, under the Jim Crow laws, Pauli would not have been able to attend school with white students. During this time it was also illegal to wear clothing that didn't match the gender on your driver's license; so Pauli likely experienced discrimination because of these things."

Ashley looked at the photo of Pauli Murray and asked, "Can we put this picture up in the classroom?"

"That's a great idea," I told her. "We are going to learn about a different person every day this week. Do you want to be in charge of displaying the photos for us and writing a caption to help us remember what we learned about each person?" I wanted Ashley to continue with this since it was her idea. In addition, even though she was an avid artist, Ashley was a reluctant writer, so I knew this kind of practice would help her gain more confidence.

Ashley nodded. She mounted the photo on construction paper and captioned it "Sometimes the words we use to describe ourselves change over time. Pauli Murray used she, he, and they pronouns."

Throughout the rest of the week, we learned about We'wha, Frida Kahlo, and Bayard Rustin. Ashley hung the photos and added captions that I helped her choose using salient quotes from our reading:

> **We'wha** — Many Native American cultures have more than two genders. We'wha was Zuni and they were Two Spirit, so they had qualities of a man and a woman.
>
> **Frida Kahlo** — Frida Kahlo was a famous Mexican painter. She was also bisexual, meaning she loved men and women. Frida Kahlo sometimes used her art to express different genders.
>
> **Bayard Rustin** — Bayard Rustin was a Black gay man and he worked with Dr. Martin Luther King Jr. during the Civil Rights Movement. He even helped him plan the March on Washington.

The captions we used were more about identities. This is mostly due to the limited amount of time we had for this unit and the complicated nature of intersectionality, but we continued to circle back to it throughout the year. I have found that complicated topics are best taught in a recursive manner so that students grapple with them in multiple contexts. Later in the year, for example, we did a unit focusing on Ella Baker, learning about her work as an activist in the Civil Rights Movement as we read the picture book *We Who Believe in Freedom: The Life and Times of Ella Baker* by Lea Williams. We discussed the ways Baker's identities as a Black woman influenced her experiences and activism. After reading about the ways she was excluded from leadership in the Southern Christian Leadership Conference, Mason raised his hand and said, "Wait a minute. Ella Baker is treated bad because she's a woman and because she's Black. That isn't fair." Realizations like this that are shared with the class community allow us to circle back to revisit intersectionality in new contexts.

TOWARD AN INCLUSIVE PRIDE FLAG

In addition to trying to talk about intersectionality by introducing individual queer activists, I wanted students to see how the Pride movement had grown more inclusive over time. I had recently read a lesson about Philadelphia's More Color More Pride campaign, where Amber Hikes and other queer activists of color called attention to the ways people of color have been historically and systemically excluded from Pride events (see Resources). To further our understanding of intersectional oppression and queerness, as well as pride and solidarity, I wanted students to learn about the significance of the rainbow flag and why it has evolved over time.

When one of my colleagues mentioned the idea of making a pride flag for our class based on a lesson from the Human Rights Campaign Foundation's Welcoming Schools program (see Resources), I realized we could center intersectional queerness by talking about how Gilbert Baker's pride flag has been adapted by contemporary activists.

We started by reading the picture book *Pride: The Story of Harvey Milk and the Rainbow Flag,* which covers some of the history behind the Gay Liberation Movement through the story of Gilbert Baker's making of the pride flag. However, if left as a stand-alone text, it can leave students thinking that the movement was started solely by white gay men. Sometimes when I know a book will require more context, I read it aloud, end with one to two discussion questions, and know that we will explore a complicated topic more in depth in the coming days.

"Why do you think the pride flag was so important?" I asked as I closed the book.

"Each stripe meant something," said Virginia.

"Yeah, and it helps people remember to celebrate who they are," Mason added.

"OK," I started, "so who do we think the pride flag is for? Why is it used?"

There was a pause. I wondered if my questions were confusing.

"It's for LGBTQ people," Nora said.

"I think it's for everybody," Virginia countered.

Knowing that this would help us start our discussion of Philadelphia's pride flag, I said, "We are going to pause here, but I want us to keep thinking about what the pride flag represents and why we have continued using it."

The next day I read *Stonewall: A Building. An Uprising. A Revolution.* to the class. This picture book tells the story of the Stonewall Inn through the perspective of the building as it changed over time. The story begins with horses in a barn stall, and then goes through the evolution of the building and its place in Greenwich Village as New York changed. The majority of the book focuses on the Stonewall Inn as a place of refuge and resilience for people in LGBTQ communities.

As I closed the book, I allowed the story to sink in before starting a reflection discussion. Virginia broke the silence. "I still don't understand why the police kept coming back."

"Because they didn't like that they were gay," retorted Asim.

"I wouldn't let them kick me out," said Mason.

"If the police didn't raid the Stonewall Inn, then we wouldn't have Pride," Ashley added.

As with *Pride*, *Stonewall* also falls short of illustrating the full history of the Stonewall uprising. Based on my students' discussion, the entire Gay Liberation Movement was getting boiled down to a few police raids at Stonewall. In actuality, many years before Stonewall, trans women of color had begun to protest the police brutality experienced by LGBTQ+ people.

One of my co-teachers came across the video *A Trans History: Time Marches Forward and So Do We*, narrated by Laverne Cox. This video describes how trans women of color started fighting for their rights at Compton's Cafeteria before the Stonewall Riots and highlights the current ongoing oppression of the trans community. Even in our short unit, I wanted students to see the influence of trans women of color in queer history and understand how trans people were purposely excluded, even erased in the dominant narrative about the origins of pride, yet are incredibly resilient.

I wanted students to see the influence of trans women of color in queer history.

I introduced the video by connecting it back to the Stonewall Inn. "Remember, Stonewall was a place for LGBTQ people to gather safely, but sometimes police would kick people out. The video we are about to watch will start with Stonewall, but then show us what happened to lead up to the uprising we know as the Stonewall Riots. This video will also help us make connections to life today."

During the video, students gasped as they noted that North Carolina was one of the states with anti-trans bills. I was glad they were making connections.

The next afternoon during literacy block I shared "Controversy Flies Over Philadelphia's New Pride Flag," an NBC News article about Philadelphia's new pride flag and their More Color More Pride campaign. I reminded students about our previous learning: "Remember how we read about Gilbert Baker's pride flag? A group of people in Philadelphia have created a new version of that flag to be more inclusive of people of color. This new flag has black and brown stripes at the top. We are going to read this article with our reading partners and then come back together to talk about it."

After reading about the newer version of the flag, Ashley suggested that we make our own Philadelphia pride flag. We pulled out paints and butcher paper, and Ashley suggested we paint handprints in a line to make the stripes. Mason quickly jumped in and drew guidelines for everyone to paint within. Nora then worked with other classmates and started crafting a letter to the co-directors to ask permission to display our work in the school lobby. A few days later, the students' request was approved and the flag was displayed in the school lobby along with a description of its history, and it stands as a reminder to students to see and celebrate the intersectional identities in our school community and understand their histories.

JUST THE BEGINNING

Throughout the year, we continued to circle back to the identity tree and intersectional queerness. Black Lives Matter Week of Action has resources on being queer and trans affirming. We talked about Janelle Monáe during our unit on Afrofuturism so that students see Afrofuturism as an example of reimagining the narrative of people of African descent outside of the heteronormativity and cissexism that were introduced and policed through colonization. Afrofuturism and the work of artists like Janelle Monáe imagines a past, present, and future where the brilliance and creativity of Black people thrives. In our unit on immigration, we read poems by undocumented queer immigrants to understand how queer immigrants experience additional challenges of acceptance and belonging due to heteronormativity in addition to xenophobia.

Centralizing intersectional queerness makes LGBTQ identities another visible part of the human experience. It helps create a classroom culture where students feel they can celebrate and express all of their identities. ●

Laura Shelton (she/they) is a white, queer person from Southern Appalachia. She is a former elementary teacher and a PhD candidate at the University of Houston. Their work focuses on justice-oriented teaching and teacher education.

RESOURCES

ACLU. 2017. *A Trans History: Time Marches Forward and So Do We.* www.aclu.org/video/trans-history-time-marches-forward-and-so-do-we

Compton, Julie. 2017. "Controversy Flies Over Philadelphia's New Pride Flag." NBC News.

GLSEN. "Solidarity Week Elementary Educator Guide." www.glsen.org/programs/solidarity-week.

Human Rights Campaign Foundation Welcoming Schools. www.welcomingschools.org/resources/lessons.

Human Rights Campaign Foundation. "Harvey Milk and the Rainbow Flag Symbols of Us: Identity Capes or Flags." Welcoming Schools. assets2.hrc.org/welcoming-schools/documents/WS_Lesson_Harvey_Milk_Rainbow_Flag_Symbols.pdf

Johnson, Chelsea; Council, LaToya; and Carolyn Choi. 2019. *IntersectionAllies: We Make Room for All.* Dottir Press.

Safir, Shane. 2016. "Fostering Identity Safety in Your Classroom." Edutopia. www.edutopia.org/blog/fostering-identity-safety-in-classroom-shane-safir.

Sanders, Rob. 2018. *Pride: The Story of Harvey Milk and the Rainbow Flag.* Random House.

Sanders, Rob. 2019. *Stonewall: A Building. An Uprising. A Revolution.* Random House.

Williams, Lea E. 2017. *We Who Believe in Freedom: The Life and Times of Ella Baker.* UNC Press Books.

BEC YOUNG

DIVERSITY IS WHAT MAKES IT INTERESTING TO STUDY LIVING THINGS

TEACHING GENDER DIVERSITY IN BIOLOGY

BY SAM LONG

I was raised the child of scientists. Science had always been an ally and a comfort, and science was never used against me — not until my junior year of high school.

It was fall 2007 and I had just come out as a transgender boy. In my newly shorn hair and baggy jeans, I sat down with my school's assistant principal to discuss the logistics of my transition.

Could I use the boys' bathroom? "No, you're not biologically a boy."

Could I use the girls' bathroom? "No, your appearance may scare the other girls."

Could I use the single-stall bathroom near the main office? "No, that's only for staff."

The message was clear: Biological or anatomical traits outweigh personal conviction in deciding whether someone is male or female. People who transgress the gender binary are scary, and they don't deserve access to the same education as others.

These days, more than a decade later, people who transgress gender norms are still marginalized, and the excuse is often the same, oversimplified appeal to "biology." Trans people are told to stay out of public restrooms, a restriction that often amounts to avoiding public life altogether, all for the supposed comfort and safety of "biological" women and men. Intersex and trans female athletes are barred from competition amid unfounded concerns that their "male" physiology provides an unfair advantage. A total of 17 states require a trans person to undergo surgery before amending the gender marker on their birth certificate. Three states outright refuse to amend an M to an F or vice versa.

These practices all treat gender, in a scientific sense, as a rigid and immutable binary.

But I am now a high school biology teacher and I know that true, complete biology is incredibly diverse.

The biology classroom has more than enough room to include and celebrate all genders. Like most teachers, I feel the pressure to get through my curriculum and prepare for standardized tests. But when I teach about the complexities of gender, I generate authentic student engagement that drives learning throughout the year.

LANGUAGE MATTERS

When we talk about gender in our classrooms, the words that we use can shape the ideas that students take away. It is useful for the class to discuss key terms and agree upon explicit definitions in advance of using the language in an academic context.

As I planned out my genetics unit for the winter quarter, I knew that gendered language would come up in almost every lesson. So I front-loaded some of those conversations. On the first day of the unit, I wrote a statement on the board: "I got half my DNA from my mom and half from my dad." For most of my 9th graders, this was either a review of middle school science, or it was knowledge so common they couldn't remember where they'd first heard it. I asked the class, "Is this statement inclusive? Is it true for every person, or are some people excluded?"

The biology classroom has more than enough room to include and celebrate all genders.

"Of course it's true for everyone," Jasmine blurted out.

"Really?" I asked. "It's true for every single person?"

After some wait time, Manuel raised a cautious hand. "Well, some kids are adopted so they didn't get any DNA from their parents."

Now students could see where this was going. I asked for more examples of people who are excluded. I got people with step-parents, same-gender parents, and with a little prompting, transgender parents. "So not everybody has two people in their family called mom and dad, who are the ones that gave them their DNA," I said to the class. "And that's all totally normal and common — the world has all kinds of families."

Although my students had been speaking in third person, I knew that a lot them lived with blended families and step-parents. I offered up my own experience. "My dad, who raised me and my sister since we were 3 years old, is a stepdad. We're not related by blood, but he's my dad — he's my real dad."

I told the class that when we talk about the two people who provide the genetic material to make a new person, we call them the "biological parents." Each person gets their DNA from their "biological parents." This word choice has its own connotations, and you may choose to use something different in your classroom. My colleague and friend Lewis Steller opts to have his students decide collectively on a term, such as "gene giver" or "egg contributor/sperm contributor."

I took my class through a similar discussion on the statement "Men produce sperm cells and women produce egg cells."

"Is it true for everyone, or are some groups excluded?"

Without difficulty, students thought of people who are infertile, people who have reached an age where they stopped making egg or sperm, and transgender people.

"Are transgender women not women just because they don't make eggs?" I asked the class. "Are infertile men not men just because they don't make sperm?" The class came to an agreement that producing reproductive cells is not what makes somebody a man or a woman.

"Then we will have to be precise with our language," I said. "We'll say that 'people with ovaries,' or maybe even 'people with functioning ovaries' produce egg cells, instead of 'women' produce egg cells. That way, all of human experience is included in our language."

This was not a challenging concept for my students. Later in the same lesson, to check for understanding, I asked Joel, "And where do these chromosomes come from?"

"From the egg and the sperm," Joel responded without pause. Not "From the mom and the dad." He had internalized a language for genetics that was both inclusive and rigorous.

FROM PATHOLOGY TO PRIDE

All through our genetics unit, I thought about how our language directs what we think of as normal or abnormal. When a student brought up mutations, which we hadn't officially covered yet, I described a mutation as a "mistake" in the DNA sequence. But why should we talk about mutations, including the ones causing red hair or blue eyes, as if they're abnormal or undesirable? When the lesson on mutation came around, I made sure to define it as a "change" in the DNA sequence.

For years, students in my school have done a research project on "genetic diseases." They choose from a list of diseases caused by single-gene mutations, then report on how the mutation leads to the physiological and social effects of the disease. I push students to read blogs, watch YouTube videos, and look through Reddit forums as ways to understand the personal experiences of affected individuals rather than only learning from medical websites. I remind them often that not all online content is information and that all content has an author with their own perspective that must be interrogated before being considered a reliable source.

This year, in response to high curiosity from students, I expanded the research topic list to include some intersex traits. These occur when genetic mutations lead to the development of reproductive anatomy that doesn't seem to fit the typical definitions of male and female.

Halfway through the project, the implications of our language occurred to me. Why call intersex a "disease" when many intersex people understand it as a natural variation in human bodies? Indeed, the combined prevalence of all intersex traits is about as common as red hair. For the next year, I changed all the project documents to say "genetic trait" rather than "genetic disease."

I think this language better encompasses the diverse ways in which people experience their own DNA. Some mutations, like the BRCA alleles associated with breast cancer, are generally viewed as pathologies to be treated. Others, like the mutations causing some forms of dwarfism and intersex traits, become core components of identity and sources of pride for many individuals.

DIVERSITY IS NEVER BORING

My students show me that they are coming to think of genetic variation as a ubiquitous fact of life, and a source of endless fascination. They ask me questions about whether certain variations could exist, from variations that they've dreamt up, to powers they've seen in a superhero movie. My students are more engaged in learning about the complexity of sex determination — the events during cell division that can lead to individuals with XO or XXY sex chromosomes — than they are in the typical XX/XY sex chromosomes.

When a student asked about how twins are made, we sketched out the embryonic development of fraternal versus identical twins. For fraternal twins, the diagram shows two large, circular egg cells each being fertilized by a different long-tailed sperm cell. This creates two siblings who share 50 percent of their DNA on average. For identical twins, the diagram shows just one egg joining with one sperm, creating a zygote that divides into two cells, then four, eight, 16, and so on. When the ball of cells physically splits, we get two siblings who share 100 percent of their DNA.

I asked the class to reason out whether genetically identical twins could be boy-girl twins.

With this sketch in mind, I asked the class to reason out whether genetically identical twins could be boy-girl twins. The answer ends up being yes, with gender transition making it all possible. Actress Laverne Cox is a trans woman with a cis male identical twin who once played Laverne's character in a pre-transition flashback on the Netflix show *Orange Is the New Black*. I myself am a trans man with an identical twin sister, and when I share this fact, not a single student is bored. They want to know: "When did you know that you were trans and she wasn't?" "Is there a gene that makes you trans?" "Did you and your sister do the same things as kids? Can we see a photo?"

Diversity is what makes it interesting to study living things. By talking about gender diversity in our classrooms, we can engage minds, de-pathologize difference, cultivate empathy, and support academic rigor for all. ●

Sam Long (he/him) is a Chinese-American-Canadian transgender man and high school science teacher in Denver. He is a co-founder of GenderInclusiveBiology.com.

RESOURCES FOR GENDER-INCLUSIVE BIOLOGY EDUCATION

Barash, David P. 2012. "The Evolutionary Mystery of Homosexuality." *The Chronicle of Higher Education.* bit.ly/BarashArticle

Kremer, William. 2014. "The evolutionary puzzle of homosexuality." *BBC News.* bit.ly/KremerArticle

Maday-Travis, Lewis. "6 Ways I Make My Science Class LGBTQ-Inclusive as a Trans Teacher." GLSEN. bit.ly/Maday-TravisArticle

Dzurick, Alex. 2018. "A Culture of Acceptance." *The Science Teacher.* bit.ly/30Rh92l

Freeman, Jon. 2018. "LGBTQ scientists are still left out." *Nature.* www.nature.com/articles/d41586-018-05587-y#:~:text=Support%20from%20mainstream%20diversity%20initiatives,for%20all%2C%20urges%20Jon%20Freeman.

Yoder, Jeremy B. and Allison Mattheis. 2015. "Queer in STEM: Workplace Experiences Reported in a National Survey of LGBTQA Individuals in Science, Technology, Engineering, and Mathematics Careers." *Journal of Homosexuality.* dx.doi.org/10.1080/00918369.2015.1078632

HHMI Sex Verification Interactive: media.hhmi.org/biointeractive/click/testing-athletes/introduction.html — A site where students and teachers can learn about the history of sex verification of athletes.

interACT-Chromosome Letter: bit.ly/ChromosomeLetter — A powerful letter from advocates for intersex youth to educational providers.

Matt Gilbert's Sex Chromosome Meiosis Game: mattgilbert.net/biologygames/meiosis/index.html — Use this site to explore origins of some intersex traits.

Project Biodiversify: projectbiodiversify.org — A site with tools for promoting diversity and inclusivity in biology classrooms.

FRANCES MURPHY

WHAT IS A FAMILY?

INCLUSIVE TEACHING ABOUT GENETICS AND REPRODUCTION IN K–12 LIFE SCIENCES

BY SAM LONG

Every year I teach biology, I pass out a student activity sheet with a diagram of an egg and a sperm on it. I say, "Good morning, class. Today we begin a new unit!" One of my 9th graders will glance at the paper, groan, and say, "We already learned this in middle school."

I've heard it a million times. Indeed, reproduction is a perennial topic in life science curricula. In the Next Generation Science Standards (NGSS), some of the earliest disciplinary core ideas for K–3 are about organisms reproducing, resembling their parents, and forming groups to survive. These fundamental ideas come back year after year as older students delve deeper into heredity, evolution, and anatomy. But too often, we teach and perpetuate a scientific concept of reproduction detached from students' social identities and their diverse families.

Without a more inclusive lens, students disengage and feel left out of science. I felt this myself as a young transgender boy in a high school biology class. We were taught that "The father *contributes the sperm* to make the child," and "To have fitness, an individual must *successfully pass on their genes*." I rolled my eyes and slouched back in my seat. I knew I would do neither of these things in my lifetime, but I still considered myself to be a valuable part of humanity, a man, and maybe someday a father. And I knew I wasn't alone — many of my peers did not fit into these oversimplified statements for one reason or another: students with two moms or two dads, those born from surrogacy, adoptees, students in foster care, students with transgender and nonbinary parents, and those with no intention to have children.

Life science education must shift to include more diverse representations of human behavior and human families. This is necessary to achieve a more accurate view of the living world, to honor student identities, and to prepare young people to live in a world where conversations about gender constantly grow and change. Here, I share some strategies that I use to make this shift.

MULTIPLE CONCEPTS OF FAMILY

Early in the year, I reserve time with my students to recognize the many meanings of "family." I share a personal story as an example. My mom gave birth to me; we share some of the same genetic material and the same traits. I could call my mom a part of my "genetic family." Then there's my dad, who entered my life when I was 3 years old. We are not genetically related, and kids used to say, "That's not your real dad." But to me, he has always been my dad. And I say he is a part of my "social family." Later when he legally adopted me, he became a part of my legal family and he gained certain rights and responsibilities.

I tell my students that I am just one example of how somebody's genetic, social, and legal concepts of family may differ. Once I have laid out some of the language necessary to discuss these variations, I tell students my expectation that they communicate precisely about families, both in and outside of science class. I expect that students say "girls" when they are talking about everybody who identifies as a girl, and they say "people with ovaries" when the discussion is only pertinent to having ovaries.

Some students are eager to share about their family structures when it comes up at some point in the year. Lucas presented a research project about androgenetic alopecia where he shared his thoughts about his own risk of early hair loss. He said to his class, "I have two moms, and I'm only genetically related to my birth mom. Her side of the family never seems to lose their hair. Then last year I got to meet my sperm donor, and he still has all of his hair. So I think I'm at a low risk for hair loss. You might be at risk if lots of your genetic relatives lost their hair early."

Precise language empowers students to share as much or as little as they choose about their lives, while still being included by default in generalized conversations about reproduction.

SEXUAL, REPRODUCTIVE, AND PARENTING BEHAVIORS

One year when I was teaching a lesson on natural selection, Kiera raised her hand and asked with a giggle, "What about gay people?"

I said, "Great question." But when I started to address the topic, Kiera said, "OK, I was just kidding."

I said, "Just kidding? There are researchers spending their lives trying to better understand your question!"

She was new to my class for the second semester and she hadn't expected a teacher to entertain a question about gay people. In conversation, I found that Kiera, like many young people, was educated to think of sex, reproduction, and parenting as fused behaviors. That is, your parents are the two people who raise you, and they also contributed the genetic material to make you, and they achieved this through sexual intercourse. If you think of it like that, then the only type of sexual behavior with any scientific significance is the kind of sex that leads to fertilization. And if you think of it like that, the people who contributed the genetic material should be the only ones to raise and care for the child. And anyone unable or unwilling to reproduce in this way is not worth talking about in science.

But reality is more complex. To begin, I remind students that natural selection is a process that acts on a population, not an individual. If a behavior helps the population to pass on genes, that behavior can be expected to persist in the population, even if it does not bring reproduction for each and every individual. Distinct from *reproductive behaviors*, humans and animals also engage in sexual behaviors that do not result in fertilization, including same-sex sexual behavior. These behaviors have an energy cost but they have persisted for many generations, so they must have a beneficial or at least neutral effect on the overall fitness of a population. The Soliloquy video *Why Does Homosexuality Evolve?* outlines several hypotheses, such as the inclusive fitness hypothesis, which states that a gene for same-sex attraction will persist in a population because even though homosexual individuals are less likely to reproduce themselves, they provide significant care to the children in their extended families, with whom they share some genes (see Resources). The video also distinguishes sex and reproduction from a third type of behavior, *parenting* or *caregiving* behaviors. These acts, which increase the survival rate of an existing offspring, can be performed by the genetic parents, (gay) extended family, or other members of society.

Students can practice distinguishing diverse behaviors using River Suh's Queer Species Database, based on Joan Roughgarden's book *Evolution's Rainbow* (see Resources). This database includes phenomena like all-female lizard reproduction and fish who change sex during their lifetime. In some years I challenge students to classify each phenomenon in the database as reproductive behavior, sexual behavior, parenting behavior, or some combination. Students can also construct explanations for how non-reproductive behaviors may still confer increased fitness. For example, I have asked my class to explain why male-male swan couples who adopt an egg have greater parenting success than male-female couples. After reading a short article that gives no hypothesis for this difference in parenting success, one student proposed "Maybe the males could use their larger bodies to defend the egg from threats." Another suggested, "The male-male couple can't become pregnant again in the future, so they can devote more energy to raise the one baby." After hearing and honoring a wide range of hypotheses, I revealed the conclusion of researchers who observed the swans: Male-male couples succeeded as parents due to better access to nesting sites and a more equitable workload.

The study of animal behavior confirms and amplifies a key message for the humans in my classroom: Your sexuality is valid, you can be a parent without having a genetic relation to your child, and you don't have to reproduce for your life to have value. I repeat this message several times to rebut the dangerous idea that our worth as humans is tied to our evolutionary fitness.

MODELS OF HEREDITY

As I started my Genetic Inheritance unit, Freddy was one of my students who cried "I already learned this in middle school!" So I asked him to use a Punnett square to predict the offspring of a mating between two humans using a pattern of simple dominance. A Punnett square is a graphic organizer used to list out possible combinations of genes that an offspring could inherit. Freddy wrote out the parental genotypes flawlessly and transferred the symbols to fill in the boxes for the possible offspring. I overheard him explaining the process to his table partner: "See these letters outside of the boxes? That's the mom and that's the dad."

"Really?" I said. "That's the mom? It looks like a bunch of letter G's to me."

Freddy said, "Well, it's not the mom, but the G stands for her genes, which is the thing that matters in this question." That got me thinking about how we would phrase it in our notes the next week. I knew that not everybody has two people they call mom and dad, who are the same people who transferred genes to them. And if we were going to draw a generalized model of heredity, it had to be broad enough to include everybody — every human and every other living thing.

I settled on the lengthy but intentional labels "Alleles of genetic parent 1" and "Alleles of genetic parent 2." As we took notes, I told my students, "You might have learned to call them just 'mom' and 'dad,' but is that inclusive? Does everybody receive their alleles, meaning their copies of genes, from their mom and dad? Our social concept of parents might be different from our genetic relations. And sometimes we need to do a Punnett square for, say, mosquitos! They don't have a social concept of a parent at all — the offspring just hatch from their eggs and fend for themselves. So we're writing down general language that makes sense for any case of sexual reproduction."

For some learners, the graphic of the Punnett square implies two parents uniting. I reminded the class that sometimes those two people don't physically come together, it's only the alleles inside their sex cells that unite. Humans do this when they use assistive reproductive technology; some animals and all plants use external fertilization. So I added an alternate set of labels to our notes: "Alleles in egg cell" and "Alleles in sperm cell." Students learning this concept for the first time received inclusive and accurate language to describe inheritance. And students like Freddy, with prior exposure to the model, seemed to readily understand these refinements. I was pleased to hear them start communicating with more precise terms like "allele" and "genotype" rather than "mom" and "mom's letters."

A few weeks later, when we got to pedigree charts, precise and inclusive language again proved essential. Since most pedigrees are drawn after macroscopic observations and not DNA testing, we labeled the square as "male phenotypic sex" and the circle as "female phenotypic sex." We designated the shaded-in shapes to mean an "affected trait" rather than "diseased" or "mutant" traits, so our key could apply broadly to everything from red hair to retinoblastoma.

To describe the relationships between individuals on the pedigree, we had to consider what was not represented. From a non-scientific perspective, a pedigree chart looks like a family tree, and a horizontal line between two people implies a marriage. But in a genetic pedigree, the horizontal line does not mean they were married, had sexual intercourse, or even met — the line only guarantees that a union of gametes took place. And a vertical line may look like a couple "having kids," but in a pedigree the line does not denote a family unit in a social or legal sense — the line only represents a transfer of genetic material between genetic parents and their offspring.

After the class became familiar with the pedigree chart, I said, "Remember that a pedigree is only a model of the real world. What are its limitations? What are some family situations that a pedigree cannot represent?"

Students needed no coaxing to respond; they drew from experience.

"Sperm donors and egg donors. And surrogate mothers — they aren't genetically related to the baby, but they still carried it."

"My adopted sister. There's no way to show the tightness of our bond on this model."

"My mom had a miscarriage. We don't know what traits the baby had, but we would still want our model to include him."

I allowed students to suggest additional symbols to represent a broader range of family stories. Many enjoyed creating new visual language, and in the process, they thought of blended families, half-siblings, divorced parents, foster families, intersex people, and even more situations that might need representation. We built the consensus that a pedigree is not a family tree, and although it represents the transfer of a particular genetic trait, it never fully represents anybody's family story — not their genetic, social, nor legal family.

That was our last day in class with pedigrees, but I went home and did more research. The earliest pedigree charts were used to track the "purity" of nobility bloodlines in England. Pedigrees were later adopted to breed animals and plants, enabling the agricultural revolution. The practice also outed early transgender people and, more notoriously, bolstered eugenics beliefs in Nazi Germany. Nazis used pedigree graphics to classify a person as Jewish, Mixed, or German ancestry under the Nuremberg Laws, as well as to forbid certain mixed marriages. Today, health care professionals use pedigrees to take a family history and to give their patients the best possible advice.

Next year, I hope to give my students more opportunity to understand the complex history of pedigrees. I want them to know that the pedigree is just one way to model genetic relationships, and it is not a socially benign or neutral tool. I plan to ask my students "How can we reconcile the utility of this model with its role in historical injustices?"

MOVING FORWARD WITH INCLUSIVE SCIENCE

I've enjoyed success in teaching inclusive genetics and reproduction in my own classroom, and I share my strategies with other educators through workshops and on my website. But this work has also drawn criticism. Although detractors frame my language as overly "politically correct," I frame it as an acknowledgement and honoring of all students and their stories. Critical voices have tried to incite outrage by saying that when I tell a class "People with ovaries produce egg cells," this somehow means I am erasing the word "women." But we do use the word "women" in our science class — when talking about people who are women. We don't say "Women produce egg cells" as a defining rule, just like we don't say "Tall people have brown hair" — it's simply not true all the time.

Any educator who makes inclusive shifts in their science curriculum must anticipate and respond to pushback. On the Gender-Inclusive Biology website, we have compiled responses to common criticisms (see Resources). If somebody is concerned that teaching about gender is not in the curriculum, we point to the NGSS, which specify that science teachers must use effective strategies to include students of different gender backgrounds. If somebody claims that these topics are not appropriate for younger grade levels, we highlight the fact that children recognize, explore, and learn about gender at every age — whether we teach it explicitly or not. We encourage teachers of the younger grade levels to work alongside their school's health educators to align the language and concepts taught in health and science.

In my classroom, I see students grow into better humans every year. By May, I hope that they understand why diversity is an important part of science and society. Although not every student uses inclusive language all the time, they have an awareness. They know that when somebody corrects their language or asks for clarification that it's about inclusion, not just about "offending people" or "getting in trouble." I don't try to shield my students from certain words forever — I know that Lucas, who has two moms, will see antiquated language on standardized exams and in college. But now he is better equipped to challenge that language, and he knows that there is a place for him in the sciences.

Not every student can receive the same level of inclusive education that I provide in my classroom, at least not while public education is in the political crosshairs, and curriculum bills threaten to intimidate and undermine educators. I have spoken to teachers whose goals are to swap out just a few words in their genetics unit — a change from "men" to "testes" is all they feel safe doing in their school. But that small change makes a big difference for students who are listening. And I notice small changes outside of schools; more and more conversations about abortion frame it as a "reproductive right" instead of strictly a "woman's right." I am excited for a future where life science education is relevant and empowering for all students. The living world has always been rife with diverse behaviors, bodies, and families — it is our duty to teach it. ●

Sam Long (he/him) is a Chinese-American-Canadian transgender man and high school science teacher in Denver. He is a co-founder of GenderInclusiveBiology.com.

RESOURCES

Elementary

Gender-Inclusive Classrooms Booklist
A teacher-curated booklist including many titles that feature diverse families. bookshop.org/shop/gender-inclusiveclassrooms-gmail-com

Gender Showcase K–5
A collection of short scenes about animals with diverse bodies, behaviors, and families. bit.ly/3YlfAkO

And Tango Makes Three by Justin Richardson and Peter Parnell (Simon and Schuster, 2005)
An illustrated, fictionalized account of the true story of two male penguins who became partners and raised a penguin chick in the Central Park Zoo.

Tell Me About Sex, Grandma by Anastasia Higginbotham (The Feminist Press at CUNY, 2017)

An illustrated book for ages 6–12 that teaches that sex is distinct from marriage or reproduction, and sex looks different for everyone.

What Makes a Baby by Cory Silverberg (Seven Stories Press, 2013)
A book for pre-school to 8 years old about where babies come from, which includes all kinds of kids, adults, and families.

Zak's Safari by Christy Tyner (CreateSpace Independent Publishing Platform, 2014)
An illustrated book about donor-conceived kids of two-mom families, for ages 4–8 and available to read online in English, Spanish, and French.

Secondary
The Allusionist podcast episode "Parents" by Helen Zaltzman
A 45-minute discussion with trans parents about the language of pregnancy, birth, and parenting. bit.ly/3jWseia

Animal Lives by Humon Comics
An illustrated collection of 33 ways that animals have sex, reproduce, parent, and form families. bit.ly/3YPpT7t

Diagram of Human Reproductive Process
A diagram that I adapted early in my teaching career to show the chromosomes and cells involved in meiosis and fertilization for humans. bit.ly/3RYwZ7k

"Evolution's Rainbow: A Queer Species Database of 200+ Organisms" by River Suh, based on Joan Roughgarden's *Evolution's Rainbow: Diversity, Gender, and Sexuality in Nature and People* (University of California Press, 2013).

Gender-Inclusive Pedigree Charts
Guidance on how to teach about pedigree charts with inclusive language, appropriate framing, and historical context. bit.ly/3Yy17ZJ

Inclusive Genetics Activities by Elizabeth Duthinh
Five activity sets using inclusive language and premises, developed by a high school teacher and physician. bit.ly/3KcBV6O

Pigeonetics Game by the University of Utah Genetic Science Learning Center
Students learn patterns of genetic inheritance in a game that accurately portrays sex and reproduction in animal species without conflating sex with gender or imposing human gender stereotypes. bit.ly/3xlNUHN

Secrets of the X Chromosome by Robin Ball
A TedEd video lesson using nuanced language and visuals to discuss the human X chromosome. bit.ly/3YxI3uQ

Soliloquy. *Why Does Homosexuality Evolve?* youtube.com/watch?v=UsX2vfFNPak

K–12 Materials
Drops Visual Dictionary
A web and mobile tool to facilitate talking about gender, sex, reproduction, and families with students who are learning English. bit.ly/3xoesIc

Gayby Baby School Action Toolkit
A documentary film about same-sex parented families with a separate school resource kit for primary and secondary students. The poster "There's More than One Way to Make a Family" can be useful for all classrooms. bit.ly/3Z94JSb

Gender-Inclusive Biology Language Guide
A comprehensive and living guide to talking about gender, sex, and sexuality in K–12 science contexts. bit.ly/3lwlVSR

Queerspawn Resource Project
A collection of resources that reflect the complex, authentic, and intersectional experiences of people with one or more LGBTQ+ parents/guardians.
bit.ly/3I4t8ky

EBIN LEE

WHAT MAKES A BABY, REALLY?

CO-CREATING INCLUSIVE RESOURCES ABOUT HUMAN REPRODUCTION WITH MIDDLE SCHOOL STUDENTS

BY LEWIS STELLER

"Do you think it could be true? That a scientist genetically edited a baby?"

I looked up to see an 8th grader leaning on a pile of ungraded science projects on my desk.

"I think we'll have to do more research to learn about the story. What have you heard about it so far?" We chatted for a few minutes, drawing some connections to previous learning and what we know about the possibilities and ethical boundaries of genetic manipulation in humans.

I was no stranger to these types of questions as a human biology teacher. The human body is inherently political, and reproduction brings up big questions for adolescents exploring their own family history, political views, gender identity, and sexuality. As an out queer and transgender middle school science teacher working in a liberal private school in Seattle, I felt supported by my administration and school community to integrate students' questions about human reproduction, ethics, and genetics into the curriculum. I wanted my students, mostly from white, upper-class families, to feel informed and empowered to explore those questions for themselves, equipped with a foundation in factual, inclusive scientific understanding. I also knew, as a white teacher with similar social capital as many of my students, that developing a critical understanding of these issues as adolescents could help them become more engaged and politically active adults, using their privilege and power to advocate for reproductive justice.

The case study my student had brought to my attention involved assisted reproductive technology, including in vitro fertilization (IVF). In this procedure, eggs and sperm are united outside the body to create a zygote, then re-implanted into a uterus after a few days of development have occurred. Many people use IVF to conceive, including those who have lower egg reserve or sperm counts, those who cannot or choose not to carry their own pregnancy, and those using donor eggs and/or sperm to have children.

Human reproduction is not always taught in a way that includes the many ways people come into this world, and IVF is overlooked by nearly all sex ed curricula. Too often, human reproduction (and sexuality) is taught in a separate, non-academic class, and framed primarily around heterosexual penis-in-vagina intercourse and its relationship to pregnancy and disease. I wanted to find resources that would allow my 8th-grade classes to engage with human reproduction in a more universal way — a way that every student could see themselves in and that would provide a basis for rich conversations about reproductive technology and genetics.

Thankfully, I had at my disposal the fabulous book *What Makes a Baby* by Cory Silverberg. This children's book was published in 2012 to much acclaim and excitement from folks across the spectrum of diverse families, caregivers, teachers, and kids. It tells the story of how babies come into the world in an accurate way without ever implying the gender(s) of baby creators, parents, or the relationship between those people. For example, many books about the origins of a baby talk about a mother carrying a pregnancy — however, many people are born to those who are not their parents (such as those born through surrogacy), or to men or nonbinary people who have a uterus and choose to carry a pregnancy. The book was a perfect way to introduce pregnancy and birth (including IVF) that didn't involve inaccurate and dysphoria-ridden resources that link what gametes people make (such as sperm or eggs) and their gender identity or relationship to future genetic descendants.

WHAT'S WRONG WITH "MOTHER" AND "FATHER"

Before we opened the book together, I needed to have an important conversation with my students. My dear friend Christine Zarker Primomo, another middle school teacher, started her units on genetics and reproduction with a norms-setting strategy around language that I wanted to try with my students.

I stood at the whiteboard, looking out at the 22 students in my classroom. "Today, we are going to be doing very important work. We are going to add a new word to the language we use in this classroom — and we get to create it, since English hasn't come up with a word for it yet."

I saw some blank stares. Students are rarely excited about vocabulary, let alone words that no one else uses.

"New people are made from merging a sperm and an egg. When you look in the genetics section of a textbook, you will often see diagrams that show genetic lineage that label the people who make those cells as "mother" and "father." What might be some issues with that?"

James, a cisgender boy who often had a lot to share, responded, "Saying 'mother' or 'father' seems to be making some assumptions."

I smiled. "Sure! Assumptions like what?"

Another student chimed in: "Like that the people who make you genetically are your parents. I'm adopted, so while I have a genetic mother and father, they're not the parents I live with."

Eli, a transgender student, added on. "It's also important to eliminate gendered language from the term, since not everyone who makes eggs is a woman, and not everyone making sperm is a man."

"Great!" I turned back to the whiteboard and wrote a first bullet point for our list. "What are some words we could use instead for the people who make the sperm and egg that become a person?"

"What about 'biological parent'?" one student asked.

I expected this based on conversations in previous sections. "I think we can be more creative — and more inclusive. Using the term 'parent' still implies a relationship that isn't necessarily there. What other words could we use that don't use that word?"

The students were quiet for a few moments. The first idea that emerged was "gene giver," or "GG" for short. One student, as a joke, suggested "biological person" instead of biological parent, which got a few laughs. (I pointed out that we are all biological people, especially in this class!) Biological Life Transmitters (BLTs), DNA deliverers, Makers, Creators, the list continued. Finally, a student looked up as though a light bulb had gone off in their head. "What about 'storks'? They bring babies!"

Once the list felt complete, students voted on their favorites. I read each name aloud and students raised their hand for as many of the names as they felt excited about using. In this section, "storks" won by a landslide. I wrote the word on the board as a reminder for us, along with the words chosen by my other three class sections, so I would remember to use each section's chosen term.

"Now that we have this word, we will all need to help each other remember to use it. Any time you hear someone saying 'mother,' 'father,' or 'parent' in a situation where they really mean 'stork,' speak up!" It didn't take long for the students to catch me at my own game — later in the period, I used "parent" to refer to a stork when discussing allele inheritance. A student said "Lewis!" without missing a beat, and in accordance with our class agreement, I said "Oops!" to acknowledge the mistake, and moved on.

Using the term "parent" still implies a relationship that isn't necessarily there.

Armed with our new language, we turned to the original text of *What Makes a Baby*, which is a colorful book aimed toward a target audience much younger than my teenage crowd. It never fails to amaze me how much of students' "cool" exterior melts away when someone reads them a picture book. As I turned the page to begin the story, some students moved to sit on their desks or on the floor to be more comfortable. Some reacted with laughter to pages with images of cartoon sperm and egg cells to create a baby. On the last page when the book asks the reader "Who was waiting for you to be born?" a chorus of students responded "Aww."

"All right, y'all. It's a good story, it's true. And we can see how the author took the time to create a story that everyone could see themselves in. In fact, they never even used language that needed to be replaced by 'storks,' which is pretty cool. But it's not exactly at an 8th-grade level. What needs to be added to get it there?"

"I feel like the book does a good job of being universal, but it doesn't have a lot of detail," one student responded. "Like, we've been talking about trans people, and surrogacy, and adoption . . . maybe it could talk more about those different things and explain them."

"Talk about sex!" another student called out. An uproar of laughter followed.

"I'm still confused about chromosomes and DNA and how they fit into the story. I think a book at our level should explain that and how it connects to a person's storks." I smiled, knowing that this was exactly the goal of the project I had in mind — for students to understand how genetic information is inherited in the most universal way possible.

"These are all really great ideas, friends. Thank you. I'm going to take these ideas and rewrite *What Makes a Baby* to better match the level we are at and help explain some of the details that we feel are missing from the text. In the next class, it will be your job to illustrate them." Some students looked excited. Others looked terrified. "Don't worry — you won't be graded on how good your pictures look, just on how well they connect to the story."

And so, *What Makes a Baby: 8th-Grade Edition* was born. I had decided to provide students with a base text, rather than having them write it themselves due to time constraints. While writing, I used inclusive language guidelines and help from friends to craft the text. For example, one strategy the AIDS Community Care of Montréal includes in their Inclusive Sex Ed Language Checklist is to focus on body parts rather than gender/sex terms: Instead of saying "women produce eggs," say "ovaries produce eggs." My colleague River Suh recommends moving toward descriptive language about frequency of traits, such as common, most often, or frequently, rather than using loaded language like "normal," "natural," or even "typical" (see Resources).

Throughout the year, we had worked on creating and using scientific diagrams, so illustrating the text felt like a nice capstone to showcase the ways those skills had developed since we had started in August. Images were an excellent way for students to externalize their thinking — they could clearly model processes and changes over time, focus on diagramming essential details to convey meaning, and familiarize themselves with the structure and function of body systems in a more comprehensive way.

DRAWING SPARKS BIG QUESTIONS

The next day, small groups of two to three students huddled around tall lab tables. Some searched for images online, others discussed the core of the text I'd given them. Some groups grabbed whiteboards to sketch out their ideas, others already had pencil on paper to outline possibilities. Using small groups was an intentional practice: I wanted students to process the information in a variety of modalities (verbal, visual, organizational), and also have a trusted peer to talk through these topics in a safe but flexible space. I was careful to put students together with those I knew they had a trusting relationship with, even if they weren't best friends. As they worked, I circulated and asked occasional questions like "What is the most important part of your page to show readers?" "What is the most confusing part of the text for you?" "How could you clarify that idea in your image?"

"Talk about sex!" another student called out.

Below are excerpts from the text that I created for *What Makes a Baby: 8th-Grade Edition*, along with conversations I had with student groups about researching and illustrating those passages.

Egg development — Before fertilization can occur, egg cells must mature. This happens in three steps. In the follicular phase, for most people who ovulate, hormones produced in the brain travel to the ovaries and stimulate the initial development of 15–20 eggs. Estrogen then limits the growth of all but one or two of those eggs to maturity in pockets called follicles.

The process of ovulation and menstruation is often overlooked and misunderstood in the science classroom. Each group assigned this page had riotous conversations about misconceptions they had about eggs, fertility, and menses.

"Wait — you mean the egg isn't what causes bleeding? What is it then?"

"Why is it that so many eggs develop, but only one or two mature? Is that how you get twins or triplets?"

"But how is it that birth control can stop your period from happening?"

As much as possible, I redirected students to either the text they were given or to online resources to find the answers to their questions. We practiced online research about the human body throughout the year, so they knew places to start for reliable information, such as Mayo Clinic, KidsHealth, and Scarleteen. It's an important skill for them to have in moments when they don't have a trusted and informed adult to lean on for answers. One group was amazed that it was the endometrial lining, not the egg, that caused bleeding during menstruation. Another had no idea that there were so many different hormones at work in the process.

Sarah and Denise, two cisgender girls working as a team, created a diagram that showed the relationships between different parts of the body in each phase of egg development and menstrual shedding. The cycles were shown at multiple scales at the same time: organ level, cellular level, and chemical level. To this day, I don't believe I have seen a clearer diagram in a textbook or online resource.

After an egg is mature, it can be fertilized by a sperm cell. Eggs and sperm both contain half of the genetic material in a human body cell. Once they combine, a ***zygote*** *is created — a single fertilized egg with a complete and unique human genome.*

Some of my favorite conversations in the unit focused on misconceptions about sperm. Many students had been exposed to the idea of a frenzied race to the finish line, even though most of the transit of sperm inside the body is controlled by cervical fluids and muscle contractions inside the body of the person receiving them. However, few if any of my students were aware that very few sperm made by a person with functional testes are considered "normal," and the rest of the sperm have some kind of variation that can impede successful fertilization of an egg. (It's a great way to compare and contrast the meiosis strategies of each cell type.)

This came up casually with one group illustrating this page. "Can you guess how many sperm produced by most sperm-producing people look like the textbook image you have in your minds?" I asked. They each guessed about 90 to 95 percent, wildly off from the actual number: 4 to 10 percent. They rushed online to look up images, and laughed riotously at pictures of sperm with two heads, sperm with two tails, sperm with giant heads, sperm with barely any head at all, and more. They drew a wide range of sperm types on their page. I saw a number of students stopping by to read that page in particular when the project was complete and hung up around the classroom.

Once an egg is fertilized, it starts to divide — really fast! Mitosis begins and the zygote becomes a morula, which is a ball of cells that some people think looks like a raspberry. A morula can develop in a variety of settings, including outside the human body. When fertilization happens in a lab, it is called "in vitro fertilization," or IVF.

I had one tender conversation during this unit with a student who had heard things about the "quality" of embryos produced through IVF. When an embryo is selected for implantation in a uterus in the process of IVF, it is given a two-letter grade that is based on the appearance of the cells and outer layer of the developing embryo. This student knew they were conceived through IVF, and worried that they were not very athletic or strong because of their conception process. They wondered if an embryo grade could be related to the way they felt in their body as a young adult. We talked for a while about the wide range of human diversity, and although embryo grade does correlate to the success rate of a pregnancy, it has not been found to have any effects on the babies born as a result. It was a reminder of how important it is to create an open space for students to express concerns and questions, and how an inclusive curriculum can make a big difference in how a student conceptualizes their own history and experiences in the context of science and the broader world.

Questions of ethics and reproductive justice came up many times in the three-week unit.

The longest amount of time a morula has lived in a lab is 13 days — that is because of an international rule that says you cannot allow a human to develop for longer than 14 days in a lab.

Questions of ethics and reproductive justice came up many times in the three-week unit. Discussions of IVF require considering when human life — and human rights — begin, and how to navigate challenging questions faced by scientists researching this subject. Considering the possibility of genetic editing and even genetic screening led to conversations about eugenics and the painful history of racist, ableist reproductive control.

In our unit on the cell cycle some months before, we had read excerpts from *The Immortal Life of Henrietta Lacks*, including passages that described Western science's persistent and ongoing lack of respect for Black life and well-being. We watched a video that explained the concept of "designer babies"; one researcher discussed how important it was to prevent the genocide of disabled communities, including the Deaf community, through genetic editing and selection.

"But Lewis, don't you think it's better for there to be less suffering in the world?" James asked something that is no doubt on the minds of many outwardly abled students. I took a deep breath.

As a transgender man who hopes to carry a pregnancy in the future, I have a deep and personal investment in inclusive, accessible, and legal reproductive health care.

"I can hear what you are saying, James. But let's step back for a minute. I know there are people in this room who have disabilities, even if they aren't visible. There are many people near and dear to my heart who are disabled, and proud of who they are and what they've experienced, which includes their experience of disability. You didn't intend to say this, but what can be heard in your statement reminds me a little bit of eugenics — deciding who is more 'ideal' or 'desirable' and choosing who gets to survive. While it's good to use science to alleviate suffering, many disabled people would say it is not their disability that causes suffering, but rather the ableist way the world is set up to not meet their needs — including how science views them and treats them."

The class was quiet for a few moments. Then, James asked, "So, do you oppose the right to abort a baby based on the results of genetic testing?"

Although I believe that each person carrying a pregnancy should have the choice of whether to continue that pregnancy or not, I was not prepared to speak to the complexity of the question James had asked, nor did I want my personal beliefs to take up so much space in the classroom that others would be uncomfortable sharing their own. I took a moment to decide how to respond.

"The decision to continue a pregnancy is deeply personal and unique to each person. I choose to not share my personal beliefs on this topic, but welcome you all to share your own beliefs, recognizing that we are not going to necessarily agree."

Now, living in a post-Roe world, these questions seem more urgent. As reproductive rights disappear across the United States, I find myself increasingly called to speak out about my own beliefs of individual agency and the right to fertility assistance and safe, legal abortion. If I could go back to that classroom conversation, I would likely disclose more of my personal experiences and ethics, and express a conviction that both reproductive rights should be protected and the rights of the disabled community need to be lifted up. After all, it is often the disabled community who is most at risk of losing control over their right to reproductive self-determination, as history has shown. I would hope that my own vulnerability would allow my students to do the same — though there are no easy answers to how to navigate those conversations in a way that will work for everyone.

As a transgender man who hopes to carry a pregnancy in the future, I have a deep and personal investment in inclusive, accessible, and legal reproductive health care. It is my hope that through this project, my students were able to better understand a more complete picture of how reproduction can happen. I also hope that by normalizing ways that the queer and trans community often bring children into their lives, I am opening space to understand and celebrate the many ways that people — storks, parents, and the humans they create together — create families.

* * *

We finished our book and read it out loud as a class. Our narrative was cohesive, inclusive, and supported students' sense-making around how IVF functions in the larger picture of pregnancy and birth. Though the original text had come from me, the conversations interwoven into the narrative and construction of students' understanding and engagement with these ideas meant that the story belonged to the whole group. In the following weeks, I saw students walk around the room and learn from one another's images and ideas. In the future, I want students to write their own text as well as create illustrations.

I hope that over time, more and more resources will become available for teaching students of all ages about reproductive science in an accurate and inclusive way. Until then, I'll be creating them alongside my students. ●

Lewis Steller (he/him) is a queer and transgender middle and high school science teacher interested in the intersections of inquiry, social justice, and play. He currently teaches grades 7–12 at a bilingual Friends school in the cloud forests of Costa Rica.

RESOURCES

What Makes a Baby? Reader's Guide
A comprehensive guide for teachers, parents, and beloved adults who want to read *What Makes a Baby?* with a young person. bit.ly/3YucwdT

The Macho Sperm Myth
This essay explores common misconceptions taught in sex ed that connect to the way gametes are often viewed through gendered stereotypes, and provides detail on what is actually occurring during reproduction. bit.ly/47pgZCR

Scarleteen
An inclusive sex ed resource geared toward teenagers and emerging adults. scarleteen.com

Inclusive Sex Ed Language Checklist
This set of language recommendations (and accompanying infographic) by SextEd can be a helpful guide for talking about reproduction, sexual organs, and identities in an inclusive way. bit.ly/3QzrsFL Infographic: bit.ly/3ORx2lJ

Talking to Kids About Science in a Gender-Inclusive Way

River Suh's guide expands on the sex ed language checklist, using similar principles, to general terms often encountered in the general classroom. bit.ly/3QQLSKL

Reproductive Justice Timeline: Forward Together.
This timeline explores major events in history connected to reproductive justice in the United States, including the disabled community, LGBTQ+ community, and communities of color. It is available in English and Spanish. bit.ly/3QAbuLB

The Gender-Inclusive Biology Project
A website dedicated to curating free, science-based resources for educators and students co-creating biology education that is inclusive of the wide spectrum of diversity in gender, sex, and sexuality in humans and beyond. genderinclusivebiology.com

Books

Corinna, Heather and Isabella Rotman. 2019. *Wait, What? A Comic Book Guide to Relationships, Bodies, and Growing Up.* Limerence Press.

Loveless, Gina. 2021. *Puberty Is Gross but Also Really Awesome.* Rodale Kids.

Quint, Chella. 2021. *Own Your Period: A Fact-Filled Guide to Period Positivity.* QEB Publishing.

Silverberg, Cory. 2013. *What Makes a Baby?* Seven Stories Press.

Silverberg, Cory. 2015. *Sex Is a Funny Word: A Book About Bodies, Feelings, and You.* Seven Stories Press.

Silverberg, Cory. 2022. *You Know, Sex: Bodies, Gender, Puberty, and Other Things.* Seven Stories Press.

Simon, Rachel E. 2020. *The Every Body Book.* Jessica Kingsley Publishers.

Skloot, Rebecca 2010. *The Immortal Life of Henrietta Lacks.* Crown Publisher.

FROM THE ACLU *A TRANS HISTORY: TIME MARCHES FORWARD AND SO DO WE.*
NARRATED BY LAVERNE COX, ILLUSTRATED BY MOLLY CRABAPPLE

NURTURING A RAINBOW OF RESISTANCE TO ANTI-LGBTQ+ LAWS

BY LINDA CHRISTENSEN

Laws targeting LGBTQ+ youth have skyrocketed in recent years, enveloping students, teachers, and schools in a dense, hostile fog of despair. Recent legislation attempts to censor LGBTQ+ curriculum, books, rainbow flags, to enforce binary bathrooms, to refuse to acknowledge students' chosen names and pronouns, to ban transgender student athletes in sports, to criminalize doctors and families who support transgender medical care and more.

However, according to the Trevor Project, an organization dedicated to advocacy, education, and crisis support for LGBTQ+ young people for more than 25 years, "[T]here is reason for optimism: Nearly 90 percent of harmful bills considered in 2022 were defeated by LGBTQ advocates and allies."

As an educator, I want to bring both stories into the classroom. Yes, students need to be aware of the devastating crush of new — and old — laws, but they also need to know the history and impact of resistance by "transcestors" and allies who have been fighting back against the erasure of the LGBTQ+ community for decades.

Unfortunately, even in Oregon, a state where LGBTQ+ studies are embedded in the state curriculum standards, students don't learn much, if anything, about LGBTQ+ history, literature, or science beyond a one-day sketch of gender identities in some 7th-grade health classes. When I asked students at Portland's Lincoln High School what LGBTQ+ curriculum they'd studied over the years, they raised their shoulders and shook their heads. Myron, a trans student said, "Until this unit, the only thing I learned about trans kids is suicide statistics." This curricular silence, the omission of LGBTQ+ lives and the work of queer activists, perpetuates a culture of invisibility that needs to end.

BUILDING A CURRICULUM: DO LAWS PROTECT OR HARM STUDENTS AND TEACHERS?

Blair Hennessy, a warm and wonderful social studies teacher, and I co-created and co-taught curriculum about the current "anti-gay" laws as well as the battles to defeat them. Blair's students, who range from sophomores to seniors, are enrolled in a Future Educators Pathway class at Lincoln High School in Portland, Oregon. We built a two-day unit around case studies of anti-LGBTQ+ laws that affect classrooms, and we highlighted the resistance to this legislation. Each class runs 90 minutes, allowing time to rotate through multiple activities.

"Over the next two days, we want you to wear two hats," Blair and I told students. "First, be a student engaging in the lessons, but also think of yourselves as future teachers who will be impacted by federal and state laws and policies as well as school boards and district administrators. Ask yourself: How do laws benefit or harm students and teachers? How do they protect the most vulnerable students? How did people resist?"

"RAINBOWLAND" AND MELISSA BOLLOW TEMPEL

We chose "Rainbowland" by Miley Cyrus and Dolly Parton as our opening lesson because of the controversy kicked off when the School District of Waukesha, Wisconsin, fired Melissa Tempel for speaking out against the banning of the song in her 1st-grade classroom. This delightful, toe-tapping tune encourages listeners to "make wrong things right/And end the fight" so we can all live in a rainbow land:

> Wouldn't it be nice to live in paradise
> Where we're free to be exactly who we are
> Let's all dig down deep inside
> Brush the judgment and fear aside
> Make wrong things right
> And end the fight
> 'Cause I promise ain't nobody gonna win (come on)

Before listening to the song, we told students that "Rainbowland" had been deleted from a 1st-grade music assembly and asked if they thought this song should be banned to protect children. "Highlight lyrics that might be problematic or harmful to children."

After quick-writing about whether the song should be banned, students talked in small groups. When we returned to the large group, Jason started the discussion by placing his pencil on his notepaper and leaning back in his chair. "I cannot think of a more appropriate song for a 1st-grade classroom." Other students agreed, noting lines about inclusion and connection, sticking together, making positive changes in the world.

We talked about Melissa Tempel, an award-winning, nationally board-certified teacher. Before watching Tempel's interview on *Democracy Now!* we asked students to take notes on why the school board fired her and to think about what message her dismissal sends to other teachers. Because resistance was a key component of the lesson, we added, "Also, think about why she risked her job to fight back."

During the interview, Tempel stated, "I think that these policies, like the controversial content policy, are expanding. . . . [T]eachers aren't allowed to wear rainbows in my district. We're not allowed to have signs that say 'anti-racist classroom.' We're not allowed to have anything that could be deemed controversial, although the controversial content policy does not explain what 'controversial' means, other than something that could be seen as political."

"Teachers aren't allowed to wear rainbows in my district. We're not allowed to have signs that say 'anti-racist classroom.' "

After students talked in their table groups, we opened the full-class discussion. "I just think that not being able to share that kind of music or rainbows makes LGBTQ+ students feel that they're not welcomed," said Adrienne. "I think that's kind of controversial itself and does not create an environment of supportiveness for all students. It's a very tunnel vision view."

Renée nodded and added, "Parents are harmed as well because their kids are the ones who are suffering from this. The teacher didn't even get any messages from parents questioning the song, so it seems obvious that the district made the decision without any parent input."

Blair prompted, "How do you think the firing of Melissa Tempel affects other teachers in the district or elsewhere?"

Sihaya said, "The message this sends to other teachers is that they are not allowed to critique the status quo of the district."

"This also leads to constricted curriculum," Andrew said. "Teachers will be afraid to teach about what the district finds 'controversial.' They might start self-censoring themselves. The outcome will be students not learning about other people's identities."

MELISSA *AND BOOK BANNING*

Blair and I chose the book *Melissa* (formerly published as *George*) as the second chunk in the first day's lessons to highlight the increase in book banning in recent years. I read Alex Gino's book when my grandson, Xavier, was in 3rd grade, and he read the book as part of the Oregon Battle of the Books (OBOB) competition and encouraged me to read it. The middle grade novel tells the story of 10-year-old Melissa — assigned male at birth — but knows she is a girl.

Several school districts in Oregon withdrew from the contest because the organizers, a group of librarians and teachers, refused to bow to the pressure to remove a book they knew students needed to read. Their public resistance, coupled with parent and community support, provided more reason to choose *Melissa* as a case study.

Although *Melissa* has the dubious honor of being the most banned book in 2018–2020, it does not stand alone. "During the first half of the 2022–23 school year, PEN America's Index of School Book Bans lists 1,477 instances of individual books banned, affecting 874 unique titles, an increase of 28 percent compared to the prior six months. . . . Overwhelmingly, book banners continue to target stories by and about people of color and LGBTQ+ individuals."

After sharing PEN America's statistics, I asked, "Did any of you read *Melissa* during OBOB?" Several students fondly remembered the book, but most weren't aware of the controversy. We asked students to read the first chapter, which opens with Melissa, still called George, sneaking into the bathroom to look at her stash of girls' magazines, concealing them again before her mother and brother return home. Returning to the protocol we used with "Rainbowland," we said, "Highlight anything that you think might be problematic or harmful to children. Think about why this book would be banned."

After listening to Jason and Andrew talk in their table group, Blair and I asked them to share their conversation with the class. "Part of the importance of this book is getting a trans person's perspective about what they go through, what they are sometimes forced to hide about themselves," Andrew started. "If you don't have that perspective, non-trans students get sheltered from trans people's lives. If you don't understand something, it makes it hard for you to appreciate someone else's struggle. We need these stories that are important for trans kids to have, but also for other kids."

Theresa followed up on Jason's and Andrew's insights: "If there are trans students who know that this book is banned, it might cause them to suppress their identity more, like if the school is banning a book about transgender people, they are banning their existence. That is harmful for kids to have to carry."

Desirée raised her hand and added, "Also, I was saying to my group, if you are trans and not out, then to have the class focusing on this book would feel like having a level of acceptance."

The depth of students' understanding and empathy for Gino's main character Melissa made me hope that they all become educators. Schools need teachers with big, empathetic hearts like the future teachers in Blair's class.

NEWBERG SCHOOL BOARD AND COMMUNITY RESISTANCE

Blair selected Newberg, Oregon, as another case study. Newberg is a small community located in the wine country 25 miles southwest of Portland. The school board's rhetoric echoed language used in legislation across the country to outlaw the teaching of critical race theory and LGBTQ+ curriculum and inclusion, citing teaching "divisive subjects" that cause students to feel "discomfort." Specifically, the board banned Black Lives Matter and gay pride symbols in 2021. In addition to tying a local issue to a national trend, Blair and I were inspired by the wave of activism spurred by the board's decision that brought diverse communities together to defeat the school board and their harmful policies.

Dave Brown, Newberg school board chair, told Oregon Public Broadcasting that he was not racist, and that the district needed to support "all" students: "As a school board, it's our job to make decisions that are going to be there for every single kid at Newberg High School, not just the kids that are represented in just one group — it has to be all kids."

The Newberg school board, which received more than 500 emails, continued to outlaw pride and BLM flags despite testimony from students, teachers, parents, and counselors. Ines Peña, the only person of color on the board, showed up to the meeting wearing a Black Lives Matter T-shirt and a rainbow headband. She asked for more student testimony. On Aug. 10, the school board voted 4-3 to ban Black Lives Matter and pride flags "to get political symbols and divisive symbols out of our schools," according to vice-chair Brian Shannon.

"These bans did not protect anyone. They harmed BIPOC and LGBTQ+ students' mental health, and they kept all students from learning how to be inclusive."

In response to the school board's repressive measures, Newberg farmers Erin McCarthy and her husband Jaybill built a 71' x 30' plywood pride flag on their hillside, which overlooks the high school football field. When word got out about their project, people from all over the region came to help build the flag. Erin said, "When members of a marginalized population ask for help, you just say yes." After the Black community reached out, they also built a BLM flag.

In September 2021, hundreds of activists took to the streets of Newberg, chanting, waving pride and BLM signs and wearing pride flags to protest the board's decision. ACLU of Oregon and the Newberg Education Association filed lawsuits against the district. Eventually, both groups won, and Newberg reversed its ban.

After watching two news clips we showed, Greta responded to our prompts of who was harmed, who was protected, and who resisted by saying "This legislation harms BIPOC and LGBTQ+ students." She connected Newberg to Waukesha. "This reminded me of the Melissa Tempel case. The school board was making decisions by themselves, based on their own beliefs without listening the students and community members."

Brianna added, "These bans did not protect anyone. They harmed BIPOC and LGBTQ+ students' mental health, and they kept all students from learning how to be inclusive." Later, she wrote on her paper, "These kinds of bans limit *all* students' knowledge by restricting their access to other people's experiences." Brianna's words about the bans harming all students were repeated on many students' papers and in their demands and rationales.

Thomas was moved by David Myers' words during the newscast. Myers, a Black man who grew up in nearby McMinnville, where he was one of a handful of Black students, said, "Having a BLM sign would not be political to Black children. Having that opportunity to feel a community support you is great for children."

Students observed that the work of activists didn't stop legislation from being written, but it made a difference. They noted that it wasn't just one action, it was the cumulative actions: the farmers, the protesters, many students and teachers, the ACLU of Oregon, and the teacher union. As Sihaya wrote, "The law being rescinded brings hope. Showing that protesting for people's rights is worth it."

A TRANS HISTORY: TIME MARCHES FORWARD AND SO DO WE

The ACLU's *A Trans History: Time Marches Forward and So Do We* is a four-minute history of the trans movement; one that every student — and teacher — should watch. Co-written by Chase Strangio, ACLU's LGBTQ & HIV Project attorney, and Zackary Drucker, and narrated by Laverne Cox, this brief history of "trancestors" is deftly and beautifully illustrated by Molly Crabapple. Instead of starting with statistics, anti-trans laws, and murder rates of trans people, the video starts with the defiance and resilience of the trans community, calling out trans women and femmes of color who led uprisings against the over-policing of trans communities in Stonewall, San Francisco, and Los Angeles. "[These events] remind us of our courageous history of resisting institutionalized bullying and oppression."

The history doesn't cover up the legislative and social harm visited on trans people. As the video points out, "In the decades that followed [these uprisings] trans people largely remained in the shadows quietly contributing to society. Our community was still denied employment, housing, health care, and legal protection — essentially the basic right to live. Yet even when they were criminalized by anti-crossdressing and anti-loitering laws, our transcestors, including Miss Major, Marsha P. Johnson, Sylvia Rivera, and Flawless Sabrina, survived. They all spent time in jail because they dared to be themselves."

Before watching the video, we asked students to think about the legacy of laws/policies and resistance. Students seemed to love the video. During our discussion, they echoed lines like "resistance is our birthright," "lawmakers can't erase us," and the term "transcestors." They also noted that because of anti-trans laws, trans people struggled to win basic rights, like housing and jobs. In her notes Adrienne wrote, "It was difficult for trans people to love themselves as they were constantly reminded that they are not worthy of that love, support, and acceptance." Later, when the video pointed out that harassment in schools often forces trans students to drop out, Renée returned to the word "sanctuary" from the video: "Schools should be sanctuaries where all students feel safe."

Four minutes is certainly not enough time to teach trans history; the fact that four minutes is more trans history than most students have received in all of their schooling is sobering. Students deserve to study LGBTQ+ struggles and movements in both local and national history.

TRANS STUDENTS SPEAK OUT

Renée's comment about schools as sanctuaries led us to the unit's final reading, which brought the laws and policies directly back to schools. Over the two days of lessons, these prospective teachers examined laws and policies that affected students and teachers, but they hadn't heard directly from trans students about the effects of these policies on their schooling. Ty Marshall, co-editor of *Transgender Justice in Schools*, and I had gathered testimonies from students around the country for our book.

Before the readings, Blair and I shared the Trevor Project's Protective Factors graphic that outlines the ways schools can improve positive outcomes and reduce stress for LGBTQ+ students. These include access to a GSA, access to gender-neutral bathrooms, most or all teachers respecting students' pronouns, access to sex education that includes LGBTQ+ experiences, and history lessons that discuss LGBTQ+ people.

We also shared the Movement Advancement Project graphic that illustrated a multi-colored map showing states that legislate inclusion of LGBTQ+ curriculum in their state standards. Oregon, one of the six states on the map, requires the study of "ethnic and social minorities, inclusive of LBGTQ2SIA+ individuals" as well as K–12 standards that promote "self-awareness, awareness of others, critical thinking, and understanding regarding the interaction between systemic social structures and histories, contributions and perspectives of individuals," naming "LGBTQ2SIA+ youth."

We asked, "How did the good intentions of the Oregon Board of Education play out in students' lives?" To answer that question, Blair and I distributed the trans students' testimonies. "As you read students' words, think about what you learned about policies and actions that make trans students feel safe and included in schools. Where do you see evidence of the impact of the state's standards in students' lives?"

Blair's students highlighted the transcripts and discussed them in their small groups before entering the conversation as a class. Many expressed surprise and outrage at how difficult it was for trans students to get their correct pronouns and names on record and used in class. "Just getting people's names and pronouns right shouldn't be that hard," said Lulu, "but it caused students anxiety to have their deadnames called out in class." Theresa's group noted how deadnaming, which is referring to a trans person by their birth name rather than their chosen name, and the lack of support for pronouns affected trans students. She pointed out a student's testimony:

> As a trans person, just the act of seeing or hearing my deadname is enough to make me upset. And I know this is a common feeling within the community. Many students do not have a safe place in their lives in which they have the luxury to change a given name. It's a part of ourselves we have grown out of, and hearing it is an act of disrespect to our identity. In class, specifically when there are substitute teachers, I get extreme anxiety knowing that my deadname will be read aloud during attendance. The act

of having to tell the substitute the specific situation, and why, is incredibly scary for a student who does not feel comfortable with the person they are sharing it with. This is causing students to out themselves in situations they may not be comfortable with, and often in front of all of their peers.

Adrienne followed up by discussing the student who said their pronouns were respected because they got good grades. "That's crazy," she said, "that not everybody can be respected. Just because somebody doesn't do as well in class they aren't respected in the same way."

Students also talked about how few students received any curriculum about LGBTQ+ people. Lacy's group pointed out the student who wrote, "Trans people never tend to get mentioned in class other than maybe a few sentences dedicated to transness in my sophomore health class and a day or two in my freshman year health class. My freshman health teacher was a queer woman."

Katrina spoke about the student who found a home in their middle school library. "The librarian made a space for me to hang out and be and talk. When I got my ID card with my deadname, I told her about it, and she helped make me an ID card that had my real name and I loved it. I kept it, and I still have it today." Katrina said, "It must be frustrating that you have to look for these little moments of acceptance and it's not a given that you're respected."

I had wondered how the trans student testimonies would land with these future educators. Some testimonies repeat information — e.g., the problem of deadnaming and pronouns — but Blair's students clearly felt empathy. Perhaps more than any other piece of the unit, the words of young people moved students to want to take action to make schools more inclusive. As Lacy wrote, "After reading the words of the high school students, I realized that there needs to be changes in the school system."

DEMANDING JUSTICE

When Blair and I started this unit, we asked students about the ways laws and policies harmed or protected students and teachers, and how resistance manifested itself. To bring the unit home, Blair prompted students to create a poster with five demands to make schools safer and more inclusive. She asked them to create a rationale for each demand:

- Why is this demand important for teachers and students?
- How does it ensure student well-being and a healthy learning community?
- How does this demand connect to case studies from class: "Rainbowland," *Melissa*, Newberg, Statistics, Trans History, trans students' testimonies?

Students quickly gathered their poster papers and markers and set to work with 20 minutes left in the period. Blair and I moved from group to group, listening in, thinking out loud with them about their rationales.

Some demands showed up on every poster. Some groups spent more time getting the five demands down as they talked through the evidence; a few were able to get both demand and rationales on their posters. I collapsed the common demands together with collective rationales:

1. Require all teachers and substitutes to roll call using last names.
    - It can be nerve-wracking to hear your deadname announced to students and to have to correct the teacher/substitute.
    - It's a simple change and can make a huge difference for LGBTQ+ students.
    - Require professional development regarding names and pronouns for staff.
2. Improve accessibility and effectiveness of changing preferred names.
    - It's difficult to find/understand how to go through the process.
    - Information should be shared on posters, on a school's website, on the system used to track attendance, grades, assignments.
    - Even if a "preferred name" is added, it is not effectively implemented.
3. Incorporate trans and LGBTQ+ history lessons into the curriculum.
    - Add a required course on LGBTQ+ history and current events to the curriculum.
    - Professional development time for teachers to develop LGBTQ+ curriculum and lessons.
    - Initiate a trans history day with a shorter schedule and a full day of lessons.
4. All identities must be represented in the classroom.
    - Flags, posters, BLM stickers to make all students feel welcome and able to see themselves in the classroom.
    - Display Black Lives Matter and pride flags on school property.
    - Pay more attention to including all identities in lessons.

Some variation of the previous four demands appeared on each group's poster, but other demands also surfaced:

- Students should have access to gender-affirming clothing in community closets.
- LGBTQ+ students should have access to mental health resources at school.
- Schools need more LGBTQ+ mentors and teachers.
- Schools should provide trans history books in the library and advertise them so students know they are available.

Their discussions pulled from the unit's different pieces, but the trans student testimony motivated most of their requests for change. Their thoughtful exchanges demonstrate both knowledge and heart — two attributes I hope they carry into their future classrooms.

POLITICAL IMAGINATION

"Any progressive social change must be imagined first, and that vision must find its most eloquent possible expression to move from vision to reality," wrote poet Martín Espada. "Any oppressive social condition, before it can be changed, must be named and condemned with words that persuade by stirring the emotions, awakening the senses. Thus the need for the political imagination."

When Blair and I constructed this unit, the rise of anti-gay laws and transphobia made us gut-punched aware of the need for schools to change, to become more inclusive and safer for LGBTQ+ students. What I hadn't understood, until I met Blair's class, was how important this work was for students to name and condemn the laws and bans and erasure of trans students by bringing the stories — from "Rainbowland" to Newberg, to *Melissa* and trans students — that stirred the emotions, outrage, and compassion of these future teachers.

Blair created a feedback document asking "What did you take away from this lesson that will impact you as a student and future educator? How will you use your learning as a form of advocacy?" Their comments demonstrate the importance of this work:

> It made me much more aware of the daily struggles trans students face and makes me want to be more sensitive to those kids during my internship and while working at camp, where living on the property for a whole week adds another level of stress for trans kids.
>
> I think that making the demands made the greatest impact on me. After reading the packet of the high school students' testimonies, I realized that there needs to be change in the school system and making the demands felt impactful.
>
> I took a lot away from this unit and I really hope that as an educator in the future I am not as restricted as some of these teachers. I will use my learning to advocate for those who are too scared to advocate for themselves.

As teachers we can't just wish injustice away. But we can educate our students, building on their empathy and compassion to make schools more just and more inclusive by giving them the opportunity to use their political imagination. ●

Linda Christensen is a Rethinking Schools editor, and author of Reading, Writing, and Rising Up: Teaching About Social Justice and the Power of the Written Word *and* Teaching for Joy and Justice: Re-Imagining the Language Arts Classroom.

CHAPTER THREE

TRANS STUDENTS SPEAK OUT

EBIN LEE

"YOU MAY JUST BE THEIR ONLY TRUSTED ADULT"

TRANS STUDENTS SPEAK OUT

We asked transgender students around the country to respond briefly to two questions: 1. What actions have teachers and/or schools taken to make you feel supported and welcome? And 2. What other changes do teachers and/or schools need to make for trans students to feel supported and welcome? Here are some of their answers, edited for clarity. — editors

A CHANGE THAT WOULD HELP trans, queer, and other students would be to focus on mental health. I'm not just a student and I'm not just trans or queer. I am my own person. I am a part of these communities but we, the people who make up these communities, are different. Take, for example, C, with me being S. I am a Black queer transmasculine person with more masculine traits. C is a white non-binary lesbian who is more flamboyant than I am. Our personalities are completely different as well as our experience. There is no *one way* to treat and respect trans identities. Everyone is different. The best way to respect a person would be to find out how they would like to be treated. Although something that would matter a lot to me is not to make a big deal of things. Outside of school I get enough attention. People are already curious about me and why I dress, talk, and act the way that I do. They don't take me seriously and barely show me respect in the way that is humanly deserved. I don't need another person trying to figure me out in front of the class. I think it's important to get to know the student and to have conversations

with them. I'm aware that teachers have a lot on their plate when it comes to their job, but making the effort to send out a survey and ask preferences on things isn't asking the world. It might just make someone who doesn't feel safe feel a bit better about being in that class or area. You may just be their only trusted adult.
—Stone (they, he, xe), 10th grade, Philadelphia

I'VE HAD FRIENDS BENEFIT FROM TEACHERS including the option to use a different name+pronouns in school than with parents. It's always nice to make name tents/tags/whatever that include pronouns and keep them up for a while — that way you don't have to voice your pronouns out loud, something that can definitely be nerve-wracking.

It's great to do roll call by last name if/when calling it out to the class; that way there's no chance of getting deadnamed to everyone. Not as easy — but a change I'd definitely like to see — would be making the steps to changing your name+gender in the school system either easier or explained better. It took me so long to figure out how because no one really told me anything. I just had to stumble into the office and awkwardly ask about it. Maybe there could be a short speech about it or even posters in the hallways. Or there could be a tab on the school website detailing the process.
—Spencer (he/him), 9th grade, Portland, Oregon

I HAVE EXPERIENCED BOTH GOOD AND BAD when it comes to being a trans student, but for the most, I have been generally surprised. Most teachers make it a means to have all students share their pronouns when introducing themselves, which provides a way for students to clearly express their gender identity without feeling pressure to do so themselves. Personally, as a trans masc yet feminine presenting person, most people tend to assume my pronouns if not explicitly stated, so having this opportunity to clearly express my identity to my peers has been helpful.

A subject that my school has yet to consider as big a problem as it is, is deadnaming. Being able to introduce yourself with your preferred name is a step in resolving this, however, it does not account for things like documents, attendance sheets, and student identification. Although I understand that students must be legally regarded using their deadnames at times, there are scenarios in which my school has become lazy in the support of their students.

As a trans person, just the act of seeing or hearing my deadname is enough to make me violently upset. And I know this is a common feeling within the community. Many students do not have a safe place in their lives in which they have the luxury to change a given name. It's a part of ourselves we have grown out of, and hearing it is an act of disrespect to our identity. In class, specifically when there are substitute teachers, I get extreme anxiety knowing that my deadname will be read aloud during attendance. The act of having to tell the substitute the specific situation and why, is scary for a student who does not feel comfortable with the person they are sharing it with. This causes students to out themselves in situations they may not be comfortable with, and often in front of their peers.

I have had many negative experiences with this scenario because it is dreadfully common. Students have zero way to know how their teachers or substitutes will react when they go out on a limb for themselves. In my first two years attending this school, this was the No. 1 experience I feared at the beginning of each school year. Although I have gone about changing my "preferred name" within the school system, this name does not show up on any of my documents, accounts, or identification, as though adding a "preferred name" does not matter at all.

Deadnames are not necessary to take attendance. Teachers should create attendance sheets for the classes using preferred names, and substitutes should receive these same lists. The Synergy platform should use the preferred names as provided, instead of treating them as an afterthought.

Thank you for making my voice heard.
—Kat (he/they), 12th grade, Portland, Oregon

A GOOD 75 PERCENT OF MY TEACHERS started the year by inviting students to share their pronouns, which was wonderful. As a student who uses they/them pronouns, I can never rely on people guessing which pronouns I use. Unfortunately, some teachers still don't start the year that way, and I've heard horror stories about substitutes who refuse to go over students' pronouns even when asked. Barely any substitute teachers follow the policy that requires them to take attendance by last names.

For the most part, my teachers have either used my pronouns correctly — after several months of misgendering and corrections from me — or they have simply not used any pronouns to refer to me due to confusion or a lack of acceptance or something of the sort. Once however, I had a Spanish teacher who after I told her my pronouns only referred to me using he/him or she/her pronouns. She was an older Catholic woman and had likely not been educated on what they/them pronouns are. There's a lot of work to be done in regards to pronouns.

I still consider myself lucky when it comes to pronouns because I conform to the typical image of nonbinary identity represented in the media. I was born with XX chromosomes, I have a short haircut, and, for the most part, I dress masculine. I have friends who do not conform to society's idea of their gender identity and they get misgendered by teachers and other students, even students of the queer community. It also helps me that my teachers are more willing to respect my pronouns because I receive good grades. I am also privileged as a student who is neurotypical, whose parents are both college educated, and who doesn't have to work to support their family. I have seen students who haven't been as lucky as me — including my own parents when they were students — and I know that my situation could be so much worse.

Trans people never get mentioned in class other than maybe a few sentences dedicated to transness in my sophomore year health class, and a day or two on it in my freshman year health class. My health teacher from freshman year was a queer woman. This is better than other schools around the country where transness is mentioned in a negative light.

Overall, there are places to find community among other students as a trans student at my school. This is because I live in Portland, Oregon, a city known for its LGBTQ+ acceptance, and most teachers are respectful. But there is still a lot to be done to increase that respectfulness (especially from substitutes) and increasing trans visibility in our curriculum. Although my city is very liberal, the intersection between being a queer trans person and being a person of color can be tough for me.

—Tonantzin (they/them), 18, Portland, Oregon

MOST TEACHERS ARE GOOD. You don't have to talk about being trans to be nice. You don't have to make a big deal of recognizing that someone's trans and telling them you support it. You can just act normal and that's good. It's also helpful when teachers (and other students) correct people when they misgender other people. It isn't a big deal, or it doesn't need to be a big deal, but it does matter, so teachers or students reminding one another is helpful. GSAs also help students feel like they aren't alone, and make safe spaces to talk about problems. It's also great that there are trans teachers at my school who can relate to some of my experiences.

You shouldn't ask trans kids questions about trans issues in front of the class or use them as your source of information about trans issues. Do your research and be aware of things. If teachers are being transphobic or unaware (misgendering, stereotyping trans people, asking about other trans students' experiences), they should stop doing that and try to learn more about trans people's experiences and issues. Also, not all trans kids are the same. I remember a teacher pulling aside me and my nonbinary friend during class time once. She told us that her friend's child had just come out as nonbinary and she asked us which gender bathroom the kid would want to use. We looked at each other and then told her that we have never met this person and have no idea which bathroom they would prefer to use. Every nonbinary person is different, and we don't all know what every other nonbinary person wants.

—Anonymous (they/them), 7th grade, Boston

WITH THE RISE OF ANTI-TRANS LEGISLATION and unnecessary controversy, it is no surprise that trans youth may feel unsafe in society and sometimes even in their own homes. Suicide levels in trans youth are skyrocketing with everything else as well, so it is crucial as an educator for you to provide a safe place for trans kids.

In my school it has been helpful when teachers switch the name and pronouns they use for you very quickly after you change them. This is important for a student's well-being, because using the wrong name or pronouns can be extremely uncomfortable, even triggering. Another thing that is helpful is to normalize trans identities. Nobody wants to feel like a freak and normalizing different gender identities not only makes trans people feel less strange, but educates everyone else.

Trans people and the spectrum of gender identities could be incorporated into education more. Exploring gender identity is important for kids. If we hadn't made those identity boxes in 2nd grade, I might still be suppressing a lot of feelings about myself. I am thankful for that project. Bullying is a significant problem in schools. Even if it doesn't seem like it, people always talk trash behind kids' backs or people post transphobic stuff online. There won't be an immediate end to this problem, but it can damage kids' mental health, so little steps to prevent it would be amazing.

If you accept and support us as the humans we are and help to make our middle school years not a living hell, that would be pretty cool.

—Carter (he/him), 8th grade, Portland, Oregon

I DON'T HAVE A LARGE AMOUNT OF EXPERIENCE with teachers who have made me feel supported and welcome. This year was the first year that I've ever had teachers who were openly supportive of trans youth and sought to bring them into the conversation. I am an 11th grader, and before my junior year there were very few mentions of the LGBTQ+ community in my classrooms, and if there were, they were rarely positive. Occasionally, a teacher would, at the beginning of the year when learning our names, ask for our pronouns as well, but it was always as an aside, more out of a "I guess that's a thing we do now" mindset rather than one actually trying to make trans kids feel safe. Since coming out as nonbinary, I haven't felt seen in most of my classes, and I even had to struggle through a class in which a teacher constantly mocked trans women, and had us debate whether trans women should be allowed in women's sports. (Terrifyingly, most of the class said they shouldn't be allowed.) Needless to say, my classroom experiences with my gender have not been wonderful. At least up until this year, that is. I don't know what shifted, whether I just have better teachers or whether teachers have started to actually think about being inclusive toward people like me, but this year has been significantly better. Not only am I taking an LGBTQ+ History course, in which my teacher made sure to learn everyone's chosen names and pronouns, rather than relying on the roster, but a lot more of my teachers included pronouns in the beginning of the year process of getting to know each other. I also appreciate that my English teacher, after learning that I am nonbinary, saw how it related to our topics that we are learning about in the class and pointed out how gender fluidity and being trans break the constraints of expectations and stereotypes (something we were studying earlier in the year). I wish that more teachers would bring queerness and queer topics into their lessons, like if standard history classes could also mention queer history. However, this does not mean that I want to be the example or expert on these topics in classes. Lessons that relate to LGBTQ+ topics should not

be brought up simply because there is a queer person in the room. But if there is an opportunity to incorporate mentions of gender and sexuality, not even as a whole lesson but simply as a note if it relates to the course, it would make me feel more safe and seen in the classroom.
—Isa (he/they), 11th grade, Philadelphia

IN 6TH GRADE, I KNEW I WAS TRANS, but I didn't say anything. I changed my name, and the school was supportive. Other kids were rough to me. I'm a quiet person and I don't like talking a lot or standing up for myself. My teachers have been good about using my new name. Walking through the hallways, kids have whispered the wrong name and pronouns at me. It pissed me off and I told my teacher. My teacher handled it for me.

The all-gender/everyone bathrooms we have are great, they have multiple stalls with doors that go all the way down. Everyone uses them and there is never an issue. I think that has been really good.

It's important to say that not medically transitioning doesn't make you less trans. I've seen online folks have said there are certain "correct" ways to transition. None of that makes you more or less trans. You get to pick. Trans people should know it's OK to be feminine or masculine, don't feel pressured by binaries.

When I was younger, I thought I couldn't dress femme because it would mean I'm not really trans. Just because they're dressing in a way you read as a certain gender doesn't mean that's how someone identifies.
—Chris (he/him), 10th grade, Portland, Oregon

I DON'T HAVE A LOT OF INSTANCES where my pronouns have been a problem or an issue at school. My dad has been weirded out when I told him I'm going by Nick at school. I accept that my family will call me my deadname; I wish it was different, but they're conservative. When I was in middle school, I had a nice experience with the librarian. She let me hang there and help reshelving books. The librarian made a space for me to hang and be and talk. When I got my ID card with my deadname, I told her about it and she helped make me an ID card that had my real name and I loved it. I kept it, and I still have it today.

I wish we had access to gender-affirming clothes in the free closet. I don't think last year in health I heard anything about trans folks. It was mental health education, but they weren't talking about trans and GNC (gender nonconforming) folks. I learned a lot of stuff from my mom and the internet. When I first came out, I created a lot of characters with different identities. It was on drawcast and framecast (drawing and animation apps that no longer exist) and I met a lot of queer and trans and nonbinary folks there. It's chill on TikTok too. People look in my bio to make sure they get my pronouns right when they comment. TikTok and other online spaces have been important to me to learn about terms, and identities.
—Nic (he/they), 10th grade, Portland, Oregon

SOME OF MY TRANSGENDER and queer friends tell me about horrible trans and homophobic experiences that happen to them. None of that ever happened to me. I think that's because I present pretty feminine, so people assume I'm a girl. The only "homophobic" experience I've ever had was in 5th grade. My teacher was fostering twins and had to leave school some days. One day she wasn't there and she left us a list of things we had to do, in order. The first thing on our list was to write about an important experience in our lives. We were learning about metaphors at the time, so we had to use those.

I had come out as gay, but I was still discovering my nonbinary identity. I wrote about how I felt different from other girls, how lonely I felt and how I thought I was the only gay person in my city. I also wrote about how getting a new shorter haircut had helped me understand my identity and how good it felt to get it.

The next day, when my teacher came back to school, she was furious. Apparently no one else had written the assignment that was first on the list, the one about an important experience. She asked everyone if they had done it, and I was the only one who said yes. She yelled at them all and asked me to read to her my writing. Luckily not in front of the whole class, but still, I was terrified. I hadn't expected that no one else would do it, and that I would have to read it to anyone. When I told her this, she thought I hadn't done it and was lying. I said that I did, but it was really personal. She said we could go outside and she would read it privately. I had never told many people about being gay, not even my parents. I didn't know what her reaction would be, if she was homophobic or wouldn't like it. After waiting for what seemed like ages, she told me it was good and she liked the metaphor I had put in. I relaxed. I went back to the classroom and did other work. A few minutes later, she called me to come over to her desk while she was talking with another student. She told me to read my writing to another student because mine "had a good metaphor." I was in shock. I thought she was an ally and knew that I hadn't come out to anyone. I didn't want to say no, she was my teacher, so I read it. After the first sentence I panicked and skimmed to where the metaphor was. I then ran away. It was bad having to out myself without wanting to, and having someone betray what you thought was trust. Luckily 6th grade opened up a new world of queerness. I connected with many gay and queer people and met a couple nonbinary people, who helped me discover that that's who I felt I was. They had this thing called GSA, which was all about the LGBTQIAP+ community and I no longer felt alone.

At school, teachers need to assume that you haven't come out yet, so that they don't accidentally out them. They also need to ask for people's pronouns so that you don't misgender them. Probably the most important is to know that not every trans experience is the same. We all experience different ways of discovering ourselves and you shouldn't treat us like we are all one person. This can make students feel safer, and more welcome at school. Lots of teachers do this, but it should be known everywhere and be something that seems obvious the way other things are. If we can do this then everyone can feel safe.

—Sam (they/them), 7th grade, Boston

ACTIONS THAT MAKE ME FEEL SUPPORTED by teachers or students can vary. The fact that there are gender-neutral bathrooms is great, and I love the idea. Another way is that students have affinity groups for the LGBTQIA+ community that meet during our morning meeting time as a class. It is important to know that I'm not alone in the school.

Although these are great things, there are definitely things I wish could be better. The effort for gender-neutral bathrooms is well intended but then they take them for staff. In our 8th-grade hall and one other of our four halls, the gender-neutral bathroom is for staff only, so every time I need to use the bathroom, I have to make a choice of doom. Another thing: I wish that they had a gender-neutral changing room for P.E. And my school at least talks about transgender kids, but we need more trans flags around the school. I see the all-inclusive flag or just the pride flag around, but I hardly or even never see the trans flag around.

—Will (he/him), 11th grade, Portland, Oregon

I USE THEY/THEM PRONOUNS, and I have recently come out as a trans nonbinary student at my school. So far all the people I have told have been supportive, even if they occasionally misgender me. I haven't told all the teachers at my school yet, because it can be hard to find the opportunity to. The teachers I have told support me entirely, some have even offered to talk more to me about gender in case I ever need help. What I found really helpful when I came out was that in my health class and GSA they have weekly check-ins where you can tell them any updates about your gender/pronouns. Other teachers aren't great with checking in on this. At the beginning of the year, they gave us a paper where we wrote down our preferred names, pronouns, what to use with our family, etc. but how I identified back then is different from the way I do now. I think that all teachers should check in on this more often, even if it's just a question at the end of an exit ticket or worksheet. I found it was a natural and easy way to tell my teachers and more people should do those kinds of things.

—Matilda (they/them), 7th grade, Boston

THE BEST THING TEACHERS DO (and have done) for me is to just call me by my correct pronouns/name and not think anything of it. Since teachers don't know all about who you are and how you like to present on a more specific level, calling me by pronouns/name has been the most helpful. For me, less is more. If someone calls me by my preferred name or pronouns, then I feel safe and assume that they support me fully. If someone brings it up or talks to me about it (even in a nice and supportive way) it usually doesn't help me feel reassured that they support me, and sometimes it even makes me think that they are questioning how I identify because of their interest in it. As long as someone calls me what I want to be called, there is no room in my mind for any doubts of their support.

As far as what to not do, don't bring up anyone's gender identity. A vast majority of trans people (myself included) just want to live life as whatever gender we are, not with the public label of "trans." Basically, don't reveal anything that could make anyone question the student's gender.
—Finn (she/her), 9th grade, Georgia

I ATTENDED AN ARTS MIDDLE SCHOOL WHEN I CAME OUT and it was considerably more accepting than the other middle schools in my district. My teachers were all so "in the loop" and took name and pronoun changes well. My high school only has gender-neutral bathrooms, which is great and eases the worry of what bathroom to use. My school counselor has been really supportive by helping me add things to my 504 plan that help with dysphoria and I was invited to a trans lunch group/club to build community.

The majority of the discomfort I feel at school comes from the other students around me. I feel like there isn't an understanding of who I am or what my identity even means. Lots of cis people only know that "I was born a girl but now I'm a boy." They don't seem to know the process of medically transitioning or the complexities and hardships of dysphoria. Even some of the teachers don't know what's going on — and it can be hard to explain "I'm sorry I scored poorly on my PACER test, I'm binding so I can't breathe correctly." It would be great to see some form of education about trans people, even if it's just "hormone blockers blah blah estrogen blah blah testosterone" — some way to make cis people see a little bit more of what's going on in my life and why I can't do some of the things that they can.
—Levi (he/him), 14, Portland, Oregon

CHAPTER FOUR

FIGHTING FOR THE RIGHT TO TEACH

EBIN LEE

BIG REACTIONS TO SMALL STEPS

ONE TEACHER'S STORY ABOUT USING INCLUSIVE CHILDREN'S LITERATURE

BY NETTIE HARRINGTON PANGALLO

"Please remember," a human resources representative said from behind the podium, "this is a conservative county."

After teaching for 10 years, I had relocated with my family to a rural community in central Virginia. The orientation was in a high school auditorium, and here I was, listening to human resources personnel tell a story about a teacher who lost her job because a parent insisted she didn't fit within the conservatism of the local community.

After the orientation, we teachers went back to our respective public schools. At mine, the introduction to the school year included a Baptist minister urging us to bow our heads and hold hands as he prayed for a successful school year.

To be clear, I taught alongside many inspiring educators in this community. At the same time, signs of social conservatism are embedded in all the county's institutions, and conformity to a Christian, heteronormative value system is a clear and socially enforced expectation. Local representatives are quick to protect their constituents' rights to discriminate against anyone who does not conform. They ignore the rights of those who are being discriminated against. Because this discrimination has become so normalized, many see upholding this status quo as "remaining neutral." Although this is, of course, a false definition of neutrality, it enables many to ignore issues of discrimination — a course of action that, in any event, is easier — by concluding that their supposed neutrality is a sign of professionalism rather than a moral shortcoming. It makes it easier to justify injustice. I have seen this mindset have significant repercussions in issues of sexism, racism, and homophobia.

If you had driven down the highway that cuts through this county in 2019, you would have seen signs mocking the identities of transgender students in our schools. In local Facebook groups, parents posted denigrating comments about trans children and their families. At school board meetings, community members made offensive statements about LGBTQIA+ students, pitting trans students' rights against those of "natural born females."

The message is clear: Pretend discrimination does not exist, and you will be rewarded.

When a group of teachers drafted a non-discrimination policy in response, the school board refused to include language that referred to "accepting and acknowledging students' individuality based on sexual orientation or gender identity." Refusing to name the existence of the oppressed group was characterized as "neutrality," and acknowledgement of oppressed populations was deemed "controversial." The message is clear: Pretend discrimination does not exist, and you will be rewarded. Acknowledge the existence of oppressed or non-conforming populations, and your professionalism will be attacked.

So when my 2nd-grade student asked, "What does gay mean?" my first thought was that my administration would expect me not to answer the question and refer the child to their parents. I also knew that this was why it was important to address it, particularly when the student revealed that another student had been calling children gay at recess. Avoiding the question would send a strong message to my students. I decided to address it.

A SMALL STEP

"Being gay is part of someone's identity. If someone is gay, that means they may fall in love with someone who is the same gender. Love is what makes a family, right? Well, families are made up in many ways," I said, "and many have two mommies or two daddies. Families can include a man and woman, two women, or two men who love each other and have decided to share their lives together. All families are different from one another, and every family deserves respect."

It was, I admit, a less-than-progressive entrance into the conversation than I would have used in other circumstances. This explanation did nothing to challenge the gender binary and stayed within the context of families. I chose this entrance point because it would ground the children in familiar territory. Since these students had learned about heterosexual nuclear families from infancy, I thought this might be a helpful starting point. Students could begin to broaden their awareness by synthesizing old information with new.

Many children were surprised that same-sex couples existed, but respect for all people and families seemed to resonate with them. One student mentioned that he knew a family with same-sex parents. Another mentioned that his mother's friend was gay, and another student raised her hand and said, "It's not OK to make fun of other people, especially when you're making fun of their identity. Then you're making fun of that person plus a lot of people you don't even know."

I thought it was the perfect time to take out Rob Sanders' *Pride: The Story of Harvey Milk and the Rainbow Flag.*

This beautifully illustrated book begins with Milk's famous words: "You have to give them hope. Hope for a better world, hope for a better tomorrow . . ." It describes how San Francisco activist Harvey Milk became famous for supporting gay rights and how he worked with Gilbert Baker to create the rainbow flag, a symbol "to make people feel they're part of a community. . . . Something extraordinary."

Pride is rated for children 5 through 8 years old. It is a Junior Library Guild selection, recommended for all ages by *School Library Journal.* Our town's public library owns the book, as did one of the schools in our district. The book has some shortcomings: It is not a fully comprehensive representation of many LGBTQIA+ experiences, does not offer connections to the broader movement, and lacks racial diversity. Yet it does reflect values of inclusivity portrayed in many of the texts taught in our state-mandated curriculum, which included figures such as Dr. Martin Luther King Jr., Thurgood Marshall, Rosa Parks, and Helen Keller. This was not lost on my students.

"I'm making a connection!" one of the children called out. "Harvey has a dream like Martin Luther King — about being treated like everyone else! And he's making speeches about it!"

"Yeah," said another. "And people are marching about it, too!"

A quiet voice joined in: "Someone shot him, too. It doesn't make sense to hurt someone just because you're not exactly the same."

Many children mumbled "yeah" and nodded heads in agreement.

And then a parent complained.

HOMOPHOBIA IN SCHOOLS

One mother was upset that her child knew what the word "gay" meant. She was angry that I compared Milk to other civil rights leaders. She contacted the principal, superintendent, and media. She was on the news declaring that I had denied her her rights as a Christian. Our principal told her I had "made poor judgment" and apologized. Other parents in our class who had contacted the school supported the book and the conversation; however, community members beyond our classroom saw the media coverage and many were outraged.

The principal held a meeting that morning to reveal a policy: Teachers must have "sensitive, controversial material" vetted by the school district before presenting it to students. If it were deemed appropriate, we would send a letter home ahead of time allowing parents to opt out of the lesson. Later that day, the administration sent a letter home with my students saying I had not followed that protocol.

That same year, administrators told some of our high school teachers to remove safe space stickers from their doors because they might alienate straight students.

Sadly, I know that this school is far from the only school in the country that functions this way.

There is a startling pattern of schools nationwide ignoring the abuse of LGBTQIA+ students. In 2021, GLSEN's National School Climate Survey found that 97 percent of LGBTQIA+ students heard the word "gay" used negatively in schools, and 68 percent heard it frequently. Ninety-five percent heard the phrase "no homo" at school, and 89 percent heard other types of homophobic slurs or remarks. Almost all LGBTQIA+ students (83 percent) experienced harassment or assault based on personal characteristics. However, 61.5 percent of these students chose not to report the incident, most commonly because "they did not think school staff would do anything about the harassment even if they did report it." More than 60 percent of the students who did report an incident said school staff did nothing or told the student to ignore it.

I realized this was one small opportunity to interrupt this oppression.

INITIATING DISCUSSIONS

First, I applied pressure from within the building by initiating discussions about LGBTQIA+ rights with administrators and colleagues. In conversations with my principal, I pointed out, "Statistically, we do serve LGBTQIA+ families and children." Indeed, a 2022 Gallup Poll found that 19.7 percent of Generation Z Americans self-identified as LGBTQ+. A growing awareness and inclusivity within communities means that number is growing with each generation as people who identify as LGBTQIA+ feel free to be themselves. I told our principal that although our students were young, there were certainly children who struggled with peer taunting, weaponized by gender stereotypes. Students were trying to make sense of their identity and gender expression in the confines of a community that provided no models for the many healthy experiences and lives beyond cisgender, heterosexual, Christian conservatism.

A few days later, the principal called me into a meeting with the assistant principal.

"We want you to know that you have our support," the principal said.

"You are on record saying that I made poor judgment. That doesn't feel like support," I responded.

"I apologized to the mother," she admitted, avoiding eye contact.

"Our point is, we don't want you to feel alone," the assistant principal said. Then she said, "No one is banning any books here. We just need to let parents have the opportunity to opt out of these discussions."

"This was in response to a student calling kids gay," I responded. "We don't give families the opportunity to opt out of anti-bullying lessons, so why would we in this case?"

"Well, maybe we should," the assistant principal replied.

Dumbfounded, I did not respond.

My principal went on to talk of how "many people feel that traditional family values are under attack."

"But they're not," I replied. "Families being presented with other ways of doing things is not an attack."

"Well, that's your opinion," she replied.

The next day, the librarian told me, "Think of it this way: It's just like how parents should be able to choose when their kids learn about Santa Claus and the Easter Bunny."

"You understand that your argument relies on comparing the LGBTQIA+ community to fictional characters, right?" I asked.

She ended the conversation.

I did have colleagues come to me and show support, even if in secret. Many teachers articulated support for the LGBTQIA+ community and for more inclusive literature and curriculum. One told me she had made that clear to our principal. People placed small gifts, letters, and cards at my classroom door. A former student's family brought me a pie. These gestures left me feeling both supported and relieved but also embarrassed. Creating a space where all students are represented should be a basic expectation. No gifts required.

PRESSURE FROM OUR COMMUNITY AND BEYOND

Many of my students' parents called the principal, superintendent, and school board members to voice their support. I contacted a local progressive group, who in turn, rallied parents to attend school board meetings and make public statements.

"This book is not about sex. . . . It is a book about identity, history, and human rights," one parent said at a meeting.

"We may not censor our children's education based on someone's religious beliefs," another stated.

"I would hope," said one mother, "that my child's family is not considered by your school to be too controversial to acknowledge."

I also contacted national organizations. The Southern Poverty Law Center's Learning for Justice (formerly Teaching Tolerance) division sent materials to our school board and administration. The National Coalition Against Censorship and the National Council of Teachers of English sent a letter pointing out that "books that honor LGBTQ histories and narratives are disproportionately censored in schools, chilling LGBTQ voices in the community . . . [whose] youth face serious threats to their mental and physical health." In their letter, they advocated that we adopt *Pride* as part of our curriculum, citing our school district's code of conduct, which recognizes "the importance of the dignity and worth of each individual."

Creating a space where all students are represented should be a basic expectation.

Copies of letters were sent to the superintendent, administrators, and school board members. The local progressive group found parents to read these letters at school board meetings. Local advocacy groups such as Equality Virginia and Side by Side also attended meetings and made statements citing statistics of LGBTQ student attendance, performance, and graduation rates when students were part of inclusive school communities compared to when they were not.

THE RESPONSE

The school board meetings concluded with the superintendent diplomatically recognizing that the board had heard opinions on "both sides" of the issue and thanked everyone for coming.

I have since learned that the one school district copy of *Pride* quietly disappeared from the school library. The district claims that it never owned it in the first place.

Clearly the aforementioned administrator's remarks that "no one is banning any books here" was suspect at the time. However, since then, the district's school board has explicitly voted in a book banning policy that became active in June 2023. Around 94 titles have been banned and physically removed from libraries and classrooms, and a disproportionate amount of these are BIPOC and LGBTQIA+ authors and stories. Teachers have anonymously disclosed to a local reporter at NBC12 News that librarians were not allowed to provide thoughtful discourse" throughout the process, and that while many educators have grave concerns, they are afraid to speak up because of potential retaliation.

However, because of community activism, the issue is not going away. Side by Side has offered LGBTQIA+ student support classes for the community, and an LGBTQIA+ equity session was offered for teachers as part of the district's summer professional development. The district created an equity team with teachers from a variety of schools working to develop a non-discrimination policy. As mentioned, the administration's approach was to put a blanket policy in place without naming any particular goals regarding specific populations within our community.

In hindsight, I've thought about how educational policies that don't address issues of equity limit students' access to an education that liberates and empowers them. "Controversial materials" policies ensure that homophobic, sexist, and racist ideas dictate how we teach students and future leaders.

But we can push back on policies, prejudice, and "remaining neutral." By engaging in one-on-one conversations in our schools and partnering with local and national social justice organizations, we can work toward a curriculum that honors children's natural curiosity and the healthy expression of diversity within our communities. Engaging students in conversation through inclusive literature is a small but important step. ●

Nettie Harrington Pangallo (she/her) is now in her 20th year as an educator, currently teaching and learning alongside her 2nd- and 3rd-grade students in Warwick, Massachusetts. She recently completed her EdS in Social Justice Education at UMass Amherst.

THE DAY OF SILENCE

QUEER KIDS, CONSERVATIVE KIDS, AND THE SILENCES WITHIN AND BETWEEN THEM

BY ANNA McMAKEN-MARSH

EBIN LEE

My heart is heavy after this year's Day of Silence. It's a complicated sadness; I don't feel my familiar righteousness or sense of direction in the face of homophobia. My mind is a puzzle and a knot. When students who are marginalized because of language and culture become silenced by classroom talk to support students who are marginalized because of their gender and sexual identities, what can I do? How can I bridge that silence?

My school district, in a medium-sized university town, holds a diverse mix of families. About 40 percent of our families are white, often they are liberal and wealthy; 60 percent are families of color. My school serves many East African and South Asian immigrant families from Somalia, Ethiopia, and Bangladesh, who often live in subsidized housing. My work as a white, anti-racist teacher centers around creating welcoming and safe spaces for students with different cultural perspectives. I structure my 6th-grade English classes around sharing stories and examining racism. I want my classroom to be a place where all my students are seen and feel heard — not just by me, but by one another.

In the early 2000s, even in our liberal community, it was not an easy decision to be open as a lesbian in the classroom, although the district was supportive. I wondered about students whose families and cultures were less accepting of gay and lesbian issues — I had both Christian and Muslim families, mainly immigrants, who grounded their family values in religious communities that held cultural, language, and gender role expectations that were deeply important to them. Although many of our values overlapped, acceptance of LGBTQ+ people was often explicitly disallowed.

I shared about my family with students, often through modeling writing tasks, or work about identity, and I led a Gender and Sexuality Alliance (GSA) group as well. Sometimes it was just rainbow cookies and unicorn bonding. Sometimes it was anger and frustration about gym teachers who divided class into boys and girls. Sometimes it was shy questions and new vocabulary.

The GSA planned and organized our yearly participation in the National Day of Silence. To raise awareness about homophobia and transphobia in schools, this day — organized in more than 3,000 schools around the country — invites students to be silent for a day. Year after year, students were surprised to find two-thirds of their classmates choosing to participate. The GSA visited homerooms, worked sign-up tables, and participated in the assembly to launch the day. The conversations, mostly between students, opened new understandings. They created a sense that many people believed in LGBTQ+ rights. Many people wanted to be supportive. Students often commented that they felt the tone shift after the Day of Silence. When I asked how many students heard the phrase "that's so gay" today, this week, this month, fewer and fewer students raised their hands. It was as if it had become uncool to use homophobic slurs. Over the years, more students began to share their queer identities. More students explored their gender identity and pronoun use.

Despite these cultural and school-based shifts, there were places that continued to feel like a knot of intersecting issues. Although my school is more than 50 percent students of color, the GSA has often been unbalanced in terms of race and religion. Students from white upper-middle-class families seemed to feel freer to explore their identities than students from strict Muslim or Christian families. White kids from liberal families still described feeling marginalized and frightened about their sexual and gender identities, but it was not comparable to the challenges described by queer students whose identities were affected by multiple forms of oppression — not just homophobia within their religious communities, but racism within the school and GSA community.

> **"I like my teacher. I like my religion. My teacher is gay. My religion says gay is bad."**

For example, a Black trans student from Somalia struggled with his family, but he also struggled with a mainly white GSA that didn't mirror his experience. "The GSA needs to work on its racism," he shared in a meeting one day. A boy whose favorite activity was designing and sewing dresses with his grandmother looked at me with hesitation when I asked him if he wanted to participate in the Day of Silence. "I . . . don't think my dad would like that very much." I pictured his loving father, who sacrificed so much to immigrate and raise Davide in the United States, and remembered the comments of colleagues at my school who shared his background and expectations around gender, saying that he needed to be more masculine. Everything I knew suggested that within his family and cultural context, he would need to live a straight and cisgendered life.

"Davide, you don't have to participate. This is a totally optional activity," I said gently. Thinking for a moment, I added, "One thing I do know about your dad, though, is that he is an incredibly kind and loving person. Your religion teaches a lot about love and respect." Davide nodded. "To me, this day is about respecting all kinds of people."

I don't know if Davide's dad would have agreed with me, but Davide decided to participate as an ally — he wore a sticker to support the day, although he didn't try to be silent.

Are 6th graders ready for this kind of tension? They are beginning to see that more than one thing can be true at the same time even when those things seem to be in conflict. "I like my teacher. I like my religion. My teacher is gay. My religion says gay is bad." Wheels within wheels. *The big wheel runs by faith, and the little wheel runs by the grace of God.* I love that line from the African American spiritual "Ezekiel Saw the Wheel," partly because I don't understand it entirely. I don't think it is wrong to expose students to ideas they can't square up yet. Kofi, an Ethiopian student, shared in class one day, "I support LGBTQ rights. My religion — well, my family isn't very religious, my dad is Muslim and my mom is Christian, but it's complicated — says it's not for me, like we're not supposed to be gay. But I want to support my friends who are LGBTQ. I think that's important." His ability to hold several complicated stories at one time is a sign of his social flexibility. He, like many of my students, is good at living in multiple worlds.

My Muslim colleague speaks with empathy for both LGBTQ+ people and her child, who is still stuck on the idea of gayness as haram. She says, "He doesn't understand yet. He sees only one truth. As an adult, I know, I can see how complicated it is. If a group of people are praying in congregation and the one leading the prayer happens to be gay then their prayer is still accepted, even if they aren't open about it. The whole concept is that it is not our job to search behind people's private lives. Also, we should not question their choices. I know there are many ways to be Muslim. But he can't see that yet." Another colleague speaks about "Lakum deenukum waliya deen," a verse from the Quran she interprets as "Everyone has their own choices."

This year, post-remote school and a year online, things feel a lot harder.

This year, I have heard homophobic slurs every day. The divisions between my queer students and my conservative students have become open and hurtful. A recent Haitian immigrant is first shocked, then disgusted, then verbally violent toward a nonbinary teacher. A white trans girl carries a giant rainbow flag through the halls, and a physical fight breaks out as an 8th grader tries to take it from her, shouting f-slurs. My own homeroom group is challenging. I hear six Muslim students quietly talk about how it is "haram." One of them asks us to use they/them pronouns, and then backs off of their decision. One student active in his Ethiopian Christian church asks me if I want him to pray for me. "Sure! Can I pray for you, too?" I ask. "Anna, you can't! You know lesbians can't be Christian." "Well, they can in my church," I respond, but he is off on another tangent.

The divisions between my queer students and my conservative students have become open and hurtful.

The wider political context weighs on queer students and immigrant students in ways both similar and different. Things feel less safe. Saturated in online chat rooms throughout the pandemic, slurs come easily to students during recess and hallway conversations, and sometimes my voice lands like a Charlie Brown adult. "That hurts!" "Please don't say that." "Do you know where the f-slur comes from?" "Stop." "Stop!" "*Stop!*" None of my words seem to work.

As in other years, I share about my wife and our children as we discuss identity. I share more in the fiction writing unit, where I ask students to write about social issues that touch their lives. I write a story based on my daughter's experience, about a girl who doesn't know how to tell her new classmates about her two moms. When we discuss credible resolutions, the students shrug and shake their heads. They glumly come to consensus: There is no realistic way for a kid to get other kids to stop saying "That's so gay." The only credible situation is one in which everyone feels really awkward.

I listen to them and I want to tell them a different story. But they are writing the story with their lives. The changes of the early 2000s are not the changes they are feeling.

When we organized the Day of Silence in the GSA this year, students had worries. "What if you are being silent, but other kids try to make fun of you?" "What if it causes kids to be *more* homophobic?" "What if it doesn't make a difference at all?" But, calmed by the activity of making rainbow-laden posters, they moved forward. They designed a slideshow to explain the day and rehearsed their presentations. They worked the sign-up table, where some students created signs they held up for a photo: "I am silent because I want to support my friends." "I am silent because I believe in LGBTQ rights." "I am silent because I am nonbinary and it's awesome!"

On the Day of Silence, like in past years, two-thirds of the students participated as allies or silent participants. At the end of the day, we met in homerooms to talk. Students in my homeroom were quiet.

"What did the Day of Silence make you think about? What did you notice today?" I asked, like I do every year.

"I don't know," they answered, one by one. "Nothing."

"Pass," said a Muslim student. Earlier in the week, as students from the GSA had presented, he had carefully covered his ears to block their story. "I can't listen," he said. "I'm not allowed."

I felt this disconnect deep in my body. Probably because it touches my life so closely. But also because I feel the conflict on both sides. The messages from families telling their children not to listen to LGBTQ+ stories hurts. But the separation between me and these particular students of color hurts as well. I think about a popular advice columnist, quick to tell people to cut off their family if they don't support their sexual or gender identities. And I think of a colleague who interrupts me with a blanket "There is no place for homophobia" when I describe the struggles of a religious student to support queer issues. I understand her desire to fully affirm LGBTQ+ people, but I think of my own experiences, the time it took for my family and my friends' families to come to new awareness and support. I remember my step-grandfather who started out telling my wife and me that he would come to our 'Celebration' (what we called our 'Wedding') but that we couldn't be a family, and who, three years later, was claiming great-grandfather status of our newly born daughter. Homophobia lives in all of us and permeates the society we live in. Like racism, it is not something you can bar at the door, not something that can be outlawed. It is something we have to allow into the conversation *in order to transform it.* It takes time, and stories, and love. It takes strategic and thoughtful action.

I felt the silence heavily. The silence of disconnection. The silence of students stuck between worlds.

Watching my students, the queer ones and the religiously conservative ones, the ones who are both queer and religious, I felt the silence heavily. The silence of disconnection. The silence of students stuck between worlds. The silence of being different.

What does it mean to be silenced? Who is being silenced in these conversations? Queer students? Conservative religious students? Immigrant students? White students? This moment of silence, at the end of the Day of Silence, reminds me that the fight for justice is not always — not ever — a clear and uncomplicated story.

Intersectionality is no buzzword. It means that being queer and white carries a different set of consequences for me, in this cultural moment, than being queer and Black, or queer and Asian. It means that I need to think about my assumptions about LGBTQ+ rights with a continuous awareness of how my connection to power, safety, and cultural capital affect my claiming of those rights. When my in-laws decided to leave the Catholic Church, after years of working within the church to expand acceptance for LGBTQ+ people, they were still in the cultural majority — able to shift communities without loss of language, history, and home.

I'm still here. I'm still your teacher. I still want to connect with you.

I was careful to reach out to my conservative religious students in the week following the Day of Silence. I'm still here. I'm still your teacher. I still want to connect with you. Your story matters, and your voice can be heard. But I also mentioned my wife. I also shared about some great books with trans characters. We can listen to one another's stories. We do not need to be silent.

In the GSA, after the Day of Silence, I asked the students to celebrate something from the day.

"I want to celebrate all the kids who participated. There were a lot!"

"I want to shout out my homeroom. In the fall, when I shared my pronouns, they were like 'huh?' but now, six months later, I feel like they really are engaged. They ask questions and have opinions. Like, they needed more information to get comfortable."

"I guess I want to celebrate that even though it isn't consistent with the theme of silence, I decided to honor the day by talking to my dad about being nonbinary for the first time. It went well!" We cheered.

"I want to celebrate a kid in my advisory. After the Day of Silence he asked if he could ask about my identity. I never thought he'd want to talk about these ideas, like, really talk. We all know the kinds of things he says in the hallways. But he was actually really cool about it. He listened to my stories about my cousin, and we just connected about it all."

Their words lift my sadness, even as I read the news from Florida and Texas about banning queerness from classrooms. I have seen transformation, again and again. Fighting all kinds of injustice takes time and work and endless patience. I know that being a strong and open lesbian teacher makes a difference to students struggling with their own identity. I know that having all teachers, no matter their identity, address LGBTQ+ history, literature, and activism throughout the curriculum makes a difference. I know having time to think and process helps all students. "I like that we can all believe different things, and we can still have conversations about it," one student reflected in class. "We can still respect one another."

All I can do is commit to having the conversations. All I can do is bring it up, listen, and use connection to bridge the silence. ●

Anna McMaken-Marsh (she/her) is a white, cisgendered middle school teacher in New England. She has been an openly queer educator in both private and public school settings for 30 years. She lives with her wife and children in Arlington, Massachusetts.

WE ANSWER HATE WITH SOLIDARITY

AN INTERVIEW WITH ELEMENTARY SCHOOL COUNSELOR MADI BOURDON

BY TY MARSHALL

Madi Bourdon (she/they) is an openly queer elementary counselor working in Portland, Oregon. In May 2023, Madi worked with one of her elementary GSAs to organize an event named PrideFest. Madi ran separate GSA programs within two schools in Southeast Portland, with PrideFest planned and hosted by one of the groups. PrideFest was intended to be an event for both GSA groups to attend — a way to provide a representative celebration for more than 70 kids between both schools. The after-school and optional event included activities to create an affirming and celebratory space open to everyone.

In light of anti-trans legislation sweeping the country, including "drag bans" targeting gender nonconforming performance everywhere from library story hours to school musicals, student and staff organizers of PrideFest decided to include a drag story hour to affirm the trans community. Publicized on social media, a right-wing talk show host learned about the event and made it an issue. As a result, both Madi and their co-planner Elliott Hinkle of Unicorn Solutions received threats. The school's phone line clogged with hateful calls. Madi and Elliott were also doxed, with their personal information publicized in an attempt to intimidate and silence them.

Madi worked with GSA parents and students to ensure that families received accurate information and ultimately chose to cancel PrideFest to protect her students. I asked Madi to share her takeaways about what it means to stand up for trans and gender nonconforming students in this political climate, and in the face of threats, how to care for community safety with resistance, visibility, and joy.

TY MARSHALL: What is important for educators to know about what it means to support trans students today?

MADI BOURDON: It's important for educators to know that their solidarity is more impactful to these kids than they may realize. Students are required to be at school — making it at least bearable, safe, and affirming is important to their education, and overall long-term wellness. As educators, many of us went into this profession hoping to make it better than what we had experienced ourselves while in school. But according to the Department of Education, transgender youth are more likely to feel unsafe at school and to be bullied. And some transgender students experience multiple forms of discrimination, including race, gender, or disability discrimination. I remember my time in school. And still to this day, in my own school, I hear from students of the harm directed at LGBTQ+ students. That happens at my school — a school where inclusivity and empathy are truly walking the walk. If this lack of safety exists even within a school like this, imagine how often things happen to LGBTQ+ youth who don't have a GSA at their school — who don't have openly queer educators working in their schools who are respected and loved like at mine? I think about those students, the ones who don't have all of the representation, celebration, and policies meant to protect and support them. Be the educator who doesn't need to fully understand your students to make them feel like they matter.

TM: As a member of the queer community yourself, you mention in your interview with *PrideScape* that despite threats of violence, you felt supported and affirmed by students and families. What made this possible?

MB: When information of the threats went out to both of my schools' communities, I received loads of supportive emails from families, asking what they could do to organize, and asking me what I needed to feel safe. After our address was posted online, a family from my current school even reached out and offered for my fiancée and me to stay at their house till the doxxing blew over. Another family, with a gender-expansive student in the GSA who was being targeted, paused their own lives to take me under their wing to provide emotional support, and to organize advocacy efforts to bring awareness to the situation.

However, the most impactful forms of support came from the students in GSA. During the conversation where I let them know what was going on, multiple students told me that I made the right choice to cancel the event to protect us. I felt so much guilt for taking away their chance to be out and proud with their school community, but they understood. They knew I wouldn't take something away from them without good reason.

TM: How did you and your students still celebrate privately and safely?

MB: We had what we called "PrideFest 2.0" about a month after the original PrideFest was set to happen. We separated the event from school to avoid additional threats of safety. We wanted students to know that no matter what, they still deserved the recognition and celebration of who they are, and to know that hate will never stop our community from showing up in support of each other. Portland's queer community made sure that we had an amazing makeup event. A queer couple hosted a pool party through Swimply. When looking for a venue that would affirm us and understand what this new event was meant to signify, we were so lucky to find a place that exuded Pride even before we walked in. We even had a local queer DJ, DJ Sappho, donate their time and musical genius. The queer community came together in the face of adversity. These moments and acts of care demonstrated to the kids how important community and chosen family truly is, and how our community will always show up for each other to silence hate. It was inspiring and I hope this impacted the students in all the best ways it impacted me.

TM: How did you work with the parent community at your school to support trans student safety?

MB: Thankfully, I mentally prepared myself when creating our GSA to come with some amount of pushback, given its offering at the elementary level. I was pretty strategic about how I would support the families' understanding of the queer community, youth, culture and current events. To support getting families on board, I did what educators do: I educated.

I started with a GSA newsletter to cover topics like student opinion pieces, GSA student highlights, anti-racism tips, resources and current events, queer history, icons, and definitions. This newsletter, named *The Gay Agenda*, did me no favors when everything blew up with PrideFest, but the name was meant to take the power back for the negative implications of the phrase. I stated at the very beginning of the newsletter that "I, a queer educator, felt this newsletter is a beautiful way to promote the acceptance and promotion of the real gay agenda: inclusion, love, and support for all" to intentionally call out the name and what the "gay agenda" actually means.

Then, two gender-expansive GSA students advocated for an all-gender bathroom to be created by presenting the who, what, where, when, and why of the possible addition. They even included quotes from fellow students about the need. Our admin at the time was on board, and the all-gender bathroom was created within the only single-stall bathroom in our school, closest to the 4th and 5th graders. With this addition, our parent community could visually see the new option for students, and learned more about why it was created from the poster outside of the bathroom.

Those two things made a big difference for the families in our communities, but the students as well. The wildest part of adding the all-gender bathroom was the high percentage of cisgender students utilizing it. It was never weird to the kids, it was simply a bathroom.

TM: What practical or safety suggestions do you have for adult allies working to increase trans visibility in their curriculum or schools?

MB: Know and understand the laws of your state. I am working on a slidedeck for educators that lists out the state-by-state laws to help them navigate what is and isn't going to fly.

Start a GSA if you feel empowered and comfortable doing so. Lean into the Title IX protections — that law is meant to safeguard students from discrimination based on sex. I am doing a Title IX presentation with my students soon to help them understand their own rights.

Don't hesitate to reach out for support from national and grassroots organizations. As educators, we have people willing to help and support us in times of joy and in need, but those people need to know of the need — don't silo yourself.

TM: Prior to experiencing your own threats, your GSA sent letters and support for other GSAs around the country who were targeted. How did you build this sense of connection? How do you think these connections served as a source of resiliency for your students in the face of threats?

MB: It started with learning of a queer educator who was targeted in my hometown for mentioning to her class her weekend plans of spending time with her girlfriend. From there, things blew up quickly for her online and led to her being doxxed, for simply mentioning her partner when asked about weekend plans. After hearing about her situation, I asked the GSA kids if they felt comfortable sending her some love, affirmation, and validation through handwritten letters. Of course they were happy to oblige. That situation was a major jumping-off point for our support for other GSAs and educators. From that point on, talking about what was happening in schools, for both queer educators and students, was a regular activity — not to scare them but to encourage safety and awareness.

Unfortunately, situations of targeting are common. They tend to be a "gray area" in terms of next steps and policies in school districts, and are often kept under wraps. I learned that the activist community is smaller than I had imagined, so connecting with those experiencing similar situations was through the grapevine. It was important for our GSA to send others some love from our out-and-proud crew amidst all the hate others were experiencing. The support for others served as a source of resiliency for my students when our situation happened, although I wish it was never something they had to navigate themselves. Fortunately, our GSA was never just a social space, but an entire program of weekly lessons, activities, and community-building — to be more prepared for hate when it comes, versus if it comes.

TM: Navigating safety and threats of violence has become a regular part of planning events for the queer and trans community. How do you balance needs for security with the need to be visible for future generations?

MB: That has been the lasting worry since our situation happened. Many people came to me very upset when Elliott and I chose to cancel our event, but to us, choosing to move forward with the risk to our entire school community's safety did not warrant a second thought. Security and visibility do not go hand in hand, especially for marginalized communities. Both today and historically, our community has created our own spaces to feel safe, to live and simply be, authentically.

But I never want GSA'ers or queer youth to get the idea that openly celebrating our identities is something that should be limited to spaces created by us, for us. Still, I stand firm on prioritizing safety above all. It is possible to be safe and open, but it is not something that works as an afterthought. Keeping our community safe will allow us to eventually serve as our community's living elders — something we currently lack.

TM: For educators based in states with legislation preventing anti-trans discrimination, we can make the mistake of believing we are safer than the 18 states from Florida to Idaho at the center of the fight for trans bodily autonomy. After your experience, what advice do you have for teachers about how we can continue to connect our struggles and keep each other safe across state lines?

MB: Never assume hate won't be directed toward you, or your school. I was naive in thinking that something like this would never happen in Portland, a city in a state with one of the highest populations of queer people and inclusive measures in the country. While major cities often serve as hubs to positively unite social differences, the accessibility of information online isn't limited to those in support of the work. Most of the hate we received came from outside of Portland and online, so being cognizant of your reach can be a good move.

I encourage joining spaces dedicated to connecting with queer educators. These groups can serve as a great way to get support, resources, and feel less alone in the work. It can be isolating without connection to your community, especially in spaces where the work is not universally supported. I recently joined one through GLSEN, and another through my friend SJ from @empoweredthroughequity, who hosts a queer educator cohort that meets biweekly online for accessibility reasons and serves as a support system for queer educators.

If you feel comfortable and safe to, wearing a Pride-related pin is a strong signal to other queer-identified or affirming educators, to invite connection. I have connected with so many people by simply noticing a sticker or pin on someone's clothes or laptop and making an effort to connect. It's a perfect way to initiate a conversation, and even cooler because it's an unspoken callback to our community's history of using symbols and words as codes to unify us. ●

Ty Marshall (he/they) is an 8th-year teacher, currently teaching social studies at McDaniel High School and English language development with Portland DART Schools.

BOREALIS

EXISTING OUTSIDE OF THE BINARY IN THE CLASSROOM

BY JULIANNA IACOVELLI

"I read that they're putting litter boxes in the bathrooms for students who identify as cats. Is your school like that?" Unfortunately, my aunt was not the first person to ask me a question like this. It appears that many people are under the impression that schools have morphed into transgender training centers. That even though we do not have enough money to put tissue boxes in classrooms, we funnel money into our "indoctrination" plans. That while I try to lesson plan for 100 different students with diverse learning styles and needs, I simultaneously take the time to turn them gay — or transgender. If I had the kind of time on my hands that Republicans seem to think I do, I'd be caught up on my grading.

As a member of Gen Z, I can't seem to kick the habit of living through catastrophic events. I was talking to a friend the other day about how I've never been able to discern if being 16 sucked really hard for everyone, or if I just happened to turn 16 during the infamous year of 2016. Becoming a teacher in the 2020s while also realizing my gender identity seems to have the same kind of vibe. Every day there is another piece of anti-trans legislation, another state I need to add to the list of places I should not visit, or another person screaming about schools trying to turn their kid gay. As someone who went to Catholic school until 18 years old, I can tell you that it doesn't matter if the environment is supportive or not — if you're gay, you're gay.

I knew I wanted to be a teacher way before I knew I wanted to explain they/them pronouns to every person I met. I wish I could tell you that there was a light bulb moment, or even a singular "coming out" story for my gender identity. But realizing who you are is never a clean process with perforated edges for a tidy tear.

For me, it was crumpled up first drafts with she/they pronouns and bisexuality written in pencil. It's wondering why being called one of the girls or a woman felt like a tiny ice pick chipping away at my self-image. Discovering the nonbinary identity felt like putting on a pair of glasses for the first time. This scary world that I've been dropped into, of no volition of my own, becomes a bit clearer, makes a bit more sense, and feels a bit more like somewhere I could continue living.

Being out as nonbinary in the high school classroom is a uniquely weird experience. It seems like pronouns have become the new "that's what she said" of jokes, even though using someone's correct pronouns is literally suicide prevention. While going through my college program I spent hours thinking about how I would present to my students. I spent time considering whether I would just drop my pronouns with no explanation, or if I would come out as nonbinary but not a lesbian, or if I should just change my name and move away — just start over because everything seemed too hard. While I student taught, news stories came out in my own home blue state about teachers being fired for teaching CRT or having a worksheet with the term "gender identity" on it. My cooperating teacher introduced me to the students as Miss Iacovelli and it just appeared to be the easiest solution. It took me until after Thanksgiving break to ask them to throw in a "they" every once in a while and after Christmas to take away "she" as an option.

When I use they/them pronouns and ask others to use them, I am outing myself. Obviously, this can be poorly received and even dangerous. While applying for jobs I kept finding myself in awkward positions of weighing the possible consequences of outing myself in an interview. On one hand, I never want to teach at a school that does not want me to be there. On the other hand, I knew that I could be seen as a liability, not worth the trouble, or a potential issue for parents. And it makes me angry to think that despite my experience, my philosophy, my pedagogy, and my degrees it could come down to how comfortable the admin would be with my presence. Ultimately, I decided to be open and clear about my pronouns and gender identity.

While applying for jobs I kept finding myself in awkward positions of weighing the possible consequences of outing myself in an interview.

Doing so also makes me an easily identifiable safe space for queer kids. While student teaching, I became part of my first GSA and saw modern high schoolers' outstanding courage and bravery. Of course, not all students welcome a queer teacher with open arms. I am currently working in an inner-city school with a majority Latine population. I am usually the first nonbinary person most of these students have met. According to UCLA's Williams Institute, 58 percent of nonbinary people identify as white, my race, while Lantine people represent 15 percent. While some kids choose to ignore my identity or reject it, I would always rather have them say the first stupid thing to come into their heads to me rather than a trans kid. However, most students have simply never heard of it before. But, even if not all my students get it, they will slap each other upside the head if one of them says "That's gay" — and that's progress! Obviously, there are still students who are gender nonconforming and/or queer, but isolated. It allows me to be some form of representation and to show that we are here in every community.

Being nonbinary in the classroom is not just a struggle, it's a superpower and I wanted the school I chose to support that. The kids know that they can come to me with any sort of problem or question without judgment. I insert queer joy and education in my classroom and my identity does not stop when I enter the school's doors. Showing my students that queer people can grow into happy, successful adults is one of the most important forms of normalization.

Plus I get funny stories like a girl calling me "Miss Mix," thinking Mx. was my last name, or a boy freezing up while greeting me because he couldn't decide whether to dap me up or hug me. At the end of the day, I care about my students way more than old people on Facebook, Fox News anchors, or the dumb questions my aunt asks. ●

Julianna Iacovelli (they/them) is a high school English teacher based in Hartford, Connecticut. Their article "Queer Joy in the Classroom" was previously published in the National Council of Teachers of English's English Journal.

LOIS BIELEFELD

FIGHTING FOR LGBTQ+ YOUTH AND FAMILIES

AN INTERVIEW WITH MELISSA BOLLOW TEMPEL

BY JODY SOKOLOWER

On July 12, 2023, 1st-grade teacher Melissa Bollow Tempel was fired in a unanimous vote by the Waukesha, Wisconsin, school board. Her offense: a tweet in which she criticized the district's decision to bar her students from singing the Dolly Parton and Miley Cyrus song "Rainbowland" in a school concert. Censorship of "Rainbowland" followed two years of escalating repression, from disbanding the district's equity team to ripping rainbow flags and anti-racist signs off classroom walls, banning rainbow lanyards, and pulling LGBTQ+ books off library shelves. The district even removed displays of its own Nondiscrimination and Access to Equal Educational Opportunity Policy as well as signs that read "This school welcomes you."

On Sept. 5, 2023 — which would have been Tempel's first day of school with her students in Waukesha — Tempel filed suit in federal district court against the school district and Superintendent James Sebert. Tempel is represented by Summer H. Murshid, of Hawks Quindel. The complaint alleges that the district and Superintendent Sebert "violated Ms. Tempel's First Amendment free speech rights by retaliating against her for engaging in protected speech."

Tempel, an award-winning dual-immersion teacher with 23 years of experience and National Board Certification, is a longtime education activist and advocate for LGBTQ+ youth. A former Rethinking Schools editorial board member, she co-edited *Rethinking Sexism, Gender, and Sexuality* (2016) and *Pencils Down: High-Stakes Testing and Accountability in Public Schools* (2012). Jody Sokolower, former *Rethinking Schools* managing editor, spoke with her after her termination hearing.

JODY SOKOLOWER: Before we get into the events that led to you being fired, what do you do in 1st grade to make school feel safe for kids who might be queer or trans, or who have relatives and friends who are queer or trans?

MELISSA BOLLOW TEMPEL: It's hard to describe because my practice is so embedded in how I am as a teacher now that I don't often have to think consciously about it. For example, I never address the class as "boys and girls." We read books that provide mirrors and windows, so children see themselves reflected and also are exposed to a wider reality. I look for books that don't necessarily focus on the difficulties of being queer or trans, but that include characters who could be queer or trans — and books where a character has two dads, but the book isn't about having two dads. I make sure that my students know that I don't see those things as weird or something to be surprised about. I guess the word is normalizing, but I don't like that term. I'll show them a picture of friends of mine, two women with two kids. And I don't mention anything specifically unless they ask.

Every year I ask the parents to send in a picture of their family. I print them and frame them, and they're up on the wall in the classroom. Everybody's family is there, and the children can see everyone's family, and you can say "hi" to your parent when you walk by if you want to.

JS: The problems started in 2021, right? What happened?

MBT: When COVID hit in early 2020, most schools closed, but not Waukesha. We were wearing masks, though, and there was a small group of people who didn't want their kids to have to wear a mask. So they got their people elected onto the school board. At a school board meeting in May of 2021, they voted to end the mask policy, and most of them ripped their masks off and made a big show out of it.

The next August, right before school started, the superintendent sent a directive to remove any signs that could be "controversial." Examples included "Black Lives Matter," "Blue Lives Matter," "This is an anti-racist classroom." That jolted me. Most people weren't talking about the importance of anti-racist signs to make the classroom feel welcoming, but I thought "No, this is terrifying." Probably that's because I realized deep down that it affected me personally as a woman of color, but at the time I wasn't thinking about it like that.

Then, following that directive, other people from the district were taking down pride flags, rainbow signs, "safe space" stickers, anything that could be seen as supportive of LGBTQ+ youth. In 2017, the school board had passed a Controversial Issues in the Classroom Policy, and it's so vague that just about anything can be seen as controversial. A kindergarten special ed teacher at another school in the district was suspended for refusing to take down a pride flag in her classroom.

This year, the school board changed the dress code, and now you can't wear a mask that has more than one color or a rainbow lanyard. And they created a parental rights resolution with basically the same guidelines as Florida's and Moms for Liberty: If a student comes out to you as queer or trans, you have to tell their parents. You have to call a child by the name and pronoun on their official paperwork unless you have written permission from the parents. They inventoried all the books in the classrooms and libraries, and pulled books with LGBTQ+ themes.

JS: How did everyone react to all the changes?

MBT: When we were told we couldn't wear rainbow lanyards, some high school teachers decided to wear glittery pink lanyards instead. They approached Diverse & Resilient, an LGBTQ+ advocacy organization in Milwaukee, which bought 100 lanyards for any teachers who wanted to wear them. First and foremost, we wanted the kids to know that we still supported them. We wanted to make sure that vulnerable students knew that we still had their backs.

Some of the strongest organizing against the district's new policies came from a group of parents in the district, the Alliance for Education in Waukesha, who originally came together because they were upset that the district wasn't taking COVID seriously enough. For example, if everyone in your family had COVID, but you didn't have any symptoms, you could come right to school. Without a mask. And the school board voted to decline federal funding for free lunch during COVID. So there were a lot of issues. They started out as Parents for Science, and then they became Parents for Science and Rainbows; that was their nickname for themselves. They talk to teachers to find out what teachers are worried about for themselves and for their students, because whatever's worrying the teachers is going to be even more worrisome for the students.

The older students fought back, too. Students from the GSAs (Gay-Straight Alliances) made public comments about how important the gay pride signs, safe space stickers, and flags were — how good it felt to see those when they were having darker days, and when they were feeling confused or didn't know who to talk to. [But the district didn't listen.] At the school board meetings, it was as if no one had spoken to them. When a teenager was crying about how they were so depressed they had to be hospitalized, the board members didn't even answer. It was horrible.

JS: There was already so much going on before the song. What happened last spring?

MBT: In early 2023, the music teacher was planning our spring concert. We sing songs in my classroom all the time. It's 1st grade and we're doing two languages, so we sing songs. The music teacher, who knows how much we sing, sent us a link to "Rainbowland" by Miley Cyrus and Dolly Parton as one of the songs selected for the spring concert.

But then in March we got an email from the music teacher saying that "Rainbowland" was out. The district would not allow it to be performed.

I was shocked. I decided I would tweet about it.

JS: What did you tweet?

MBT: "My 1st graders were so excited to sing 'Rainbowland' for our spring concert but it has been vetoed by our administration. When will it end?" And then the text of the song.

It got picked up and it went everywhere. This was during spring break. I tweeted on Tuesday. Friday night I saw something about it in the *LA Times*. Then I saw it was on TMZ. I thought, "Maybe I should look at my Twitter account." There were a bunch of messages from different media asking for interviews. I was excited that people thought it was as ridiculous as I did, and wanted to know more about why this was happening. I did the interviews, explaining how we couldn't have safe space stickers, or rainbows, or anti-racist signs, and all that.

When I showed up for school on Monday after the break I was met by the police, the deputy superintendent, a school board member, my principal, and someone from human resources. They told me that I was being put on administrative leave, and that I needed to give them my district-issued computer and iPad and leave. That was it. I wasn't allowed to say goodbye to the kids, and I was told not to talk to anybody about this or it would be grounds for immediate termination. On the way out I got a text from a mom, saying that her son had started a new medication over spring break. I thought, "What am I supposed to do with this? I'm not allowed to talk to anyone."

Then I was on leave, and I didn't know what was going on. The hardest part was that my students didn't have a teacher and the families weren't even given the respect of a message from the administration saying "We're sorry your teacher's out, this is who to contact if you have questions." Nothing.

I heard from parents that their kids were really affected by my absence. Because of the attack on the parade a lot of the kids were especially sensitive to change and had a lot of social-emotional needs. [In November 2021, someone drove an SUV through the annual Christmas parade in Waukesha, killing six people and injuring 62.]

JS: How did the community respond?

MBT: The Parents Alliance did a press release. They sent emails. They sent more emails. They organized other people to send emails to the superintendent and the school board. At one point I heard that the district was getting 35 emails in support of me to every one email against. I don't know how many they got in all, but according to the testimony at the hearing, they had hundreds of emails and voicemails.

The week after I was put on leave, the United Unitarian Universalist Congregation organized a "Rainbowland" sing-along at the school board meeting.

Wisconsin State Superintendent of Public Instruction Jill Underly wrote a letter to the school board saying: "You are, under the guise of protection, causing undue harm to students and staff. . . . It is paramount that you change course now." She really stuck her neck out to do that.

JS: What about the union?

MBT: The union and the parents organized a Rainbow Day in the district when students and staff wore rainbows in support of me. Without the union [Wisconsin Education Association Council and the National Education Association], I would have been fired without a public hearing. I wouldn't have been able to hire a lawyer to work with me. And I wouldn't have been paid while I was on administrative leave. So I'm definitely grateful that I am a union member, and that the unions exist. But this is a good example of why unions need to step up, because I think that a lot more could have been done.

JS: I know you got incredible support from all over the country. Can you share a couple of examples?

MBT: GSAFE, which works to ensure that trans students are supported and respected in Wisconsin schools, had a conference in April where they sang "Rainbowland" for me, videotaped it, and put it online.

Then the Stonewall Chorale, New York City's first LGBTQ+ choir, sang "Rainbowland" in my honor at their Pride Month concert. They invited me to the concert, and it was amazing. The theme was drag queen storytime. The drag queen star Temple Grandé — who is the most grande person you've ever met in your life, like 6 feet 5 inches — wore a beautiful rainbow gown and read a story about LGBTQ+ history, interspersed with songs from each era, and then the chorale ended with "Rainbowland."

When Temple Grandé said, "And that teacher is here!" everyone in the audience gasped, and then they gave me a standing ovation.

All the support makes me want to keep going. I've been given this opportunity and it's my duty to do whatever I can with it. I can't just let it pass by without trying to raise more awareness. It's a perfect storm: I've had years of experience organizing around education and LGBTQ+ rights at school. And then there's this song by two famous artists, and it was a song that nobody knew because it didn't hit the top 100 when it was released in 2017. When people see who wrote the song, they want to listen to it, and they're baffled about why there's a problem, and so that works out in our favor. In many ways, this opportunity is a gift, and I'm excited for whatever can happen for however long it lasts.

JS: What happened with your job?

MBT: The superintendent sent me a letter recommending that I be fired. He ignored why "Rainbowland" was barred and said the way I raised my disagreement was "inappropriate, disruptive, and in violation of various district policies." There was a public hearing on July 12. A couple of hundred supporters came, wearing black and carrying signs about First Amendment rights. They filled the hearing room and an overflow room.

But it wasn't a real hearing. The person running it was the school board's lawyer. And the district hadn't honored any of our public record requests, so we had no way to argue about what happened. So my lawyer asked as many questions as possible with an eye toward the next step. And the school board voted unanimously to fire me.

JS: What are the next steps?

MBT: We've filed a lawsuit with the federal district court in Wisconsin and in the meantime, I'm committed to doing as much outreach as I can. I'm connecting with other teachers and educators who have been through similar experiences.

JS: How do you see the relationship between the attacks on trans and queer youth in schools — which is really why you got fired — and attacks on teaching Black history, critical race theory, the book bans?

MBT: It's all coming from the same place. Right-wing politicians want what we can teach in our public schools tightly controlled and censored. They want to eliminate teacher autonomy so we can't do what we need to do: Teach students the people's history, give them multiple perspectives on the world, and be inclusive, accepting, and supportive of all students. These are public schools and yet we are being told to ignore the needs of our students. It's mind-blowing. ●

CHAPTER FIVE

RESOURCES

THE CHILDREN ARE SEEN:

TRANS AUTHORS AND CHARACTERS IN CHILDREN'S LITERATURE

BY LORA LYN WORDEN

When *Rethinking Schools* magazine first published "What Kind Are You? Transgender Characters in Children's Literature," a colleague encouraged me to send Alex Gino the letter I'd co-written in support of *Melissa* (formerly published as *George*) as an Oregon Battle of the Books title, along with a copy of the article. That year, *Melissa* topped the American Library Association's most frequently challenged books list and it remained the No. 1 most challenged book for three years running. Mx. Gino responded, letting me know they would be visiting Portland later that school year and asked if we would be interested in them coming to our school. Yes, we would!

At International School of Portland, 3rd- through 5th-grade students sat in rapt attention while Mx. Gino read from *Melissa*, talked about their own writing process, and led a small writing workshop. There were many highlights to their visit, including valuable feedback they offered about my article: to not only promote books about only transgender and genderqueer characters, but to promote books about transgender characters written by transgender and genderqueer authors.

The 10 books I reviewed in that article were:

- Anderson, Airlie. 2018. *Neither*. Little, Brown and Company.
- Baldacchino, Christine. 2014. *Morris Micklewhite and the Tangerine Dress*. Groundwood Books.
- Gephart, Donna. 2016. *Lily and Dunkin*. Delacorte Press.
- Gino, Alex. 2015. *Melissa*. Scholastic Press.
- Hennessey, M. G. 2016. *The Other Boy*. Harper.

- Herthel, Jessica, and Jennings, Jazz. 2014. *I Am Jazz*. Dial Books.
- Love, Jessica. 2018. *Julián Is a Mermaid*. Candlewick Press.
- Polonsky, Ami. 2014. *Gracefully Grayson*. Hyperion.
- Walton, Jessica. 2016. *Introducing Teddy: A Gentle Story About Gender and Friendship*. Bloomsbury.
- Wang, Jen. 2018. *The Prince and the Dressmaker*. First Second.

Of these titles, only two books were written or co-written by a transgender person. In addition, when publishers first started publishing picture books and middle grade novels with transgender characters, they were primarily books about transgender characters facing challenges to their gender identity: problem novels in which the main "problem" of the story had to do with the protagonist coping with friends, family, and/or teachers not accepting their gender identity. Of the titles listed above, the main character's gender identity and/or gender expression, and how others react to it, is a central conflict in nearly every story. This isn't to say these books are not valuable. They are. Books such as Alex Gino's *Melissa* and Jazz Jennings' *I am Jazz* are two early titles by and about transgender people that provide valuable insight into a young person's gender journey. I continue to use and/or recommend all of these books, but especially those two, in the elementary school library. Still, it's exciting to see even more books published that are not just stories about coming out. These stories — complex, rich, diverse — are all invaluable.

In 2018, when *Melissa* first topped the most frequently challenged books list, the American Library Association (ALA) reported 483 book challenges in the United States. In 2022, the ALA noted, a "record 2,571 unique titles were targeted for censorship." Of the top 13 titles challenged in 2022, seven titles were challenged for LGBTQIA+ content. This increased effort to silence the voices of LGBTQIA+ writers and characters, including transgender and genderqueer characters, is alarming, especially in consideration of how the increase in book bannings and anti-trans legislation impacts young people's mental health.

Books by and about transgender and genderqueer people is a great way to support our transgender and genderqueer students and families. In their 2022 national survey, the Trevor Project also reported sources of joy for LGBTQIA+ youth, which included:

- Seeing LGBTQ people of color represented in media
- Happy LGBTQ elders & married couples
- Learning about LGBTQ history
- Having a safe space to express gender, gender identity, and sexuality

- Learning that I'm not alone and there are more people like me
- Self-love and acceptance
- Queer role models
- Supportive teachers

Although there has been a dramatic increase in book challenges in the United States during the past five years, there's also been a dramatic increase in books written by and about transgender people. As an elementary school librarian, I constantly search for books to add to our collection, to recommend to colleagues and students, and to read with my classes. Taking Mx. Gino's advice to heart, I strive to find books in which students can see themselves, and others, in the people who create the books. To do this, I frequently post author/illustrator pictures alongside book covers in promotional displays in the library. I also show videos of authors/illustrators reading their own work, and encourage students to listen to audiobooks including those read by the author.

PICTURE BOOKS

Included in my repertoire of diverse family stories that I read to younger elementary-age students, are three titles featuring genderqueer characters.

When Aidan Became a Brother by Kyle Lukoff is a sweet story about a boy who is about to become a big brother, a topic many elementary students can relate to. Aidan feels protective when strangers ask if he wants a brother or a sister or if his mom is expecting a boy or a girl. Aidan, who is transgender, wants his sibling to feel welcomed and loved regardless of their gender. It is a tender story for elementary students.

With its gorgeous cover, *My Rainbow*, written by Trinity and DeShanna Neal and illustrated by Art Twink, invites readers into a poignant story that shows both a mother's love and the intersectionality of one child's identity. As a child with autism, Trinity loves the soft feel of her pet pig's hair, but cannot stand the feel of her own hair when it grows out and tickles her neck. And though Trinity understands that people of any gender can have short or long hair, it's important to her, as a transgender girl, to have long hair. As she tells her mother, "People don't care if cisgender girls like you have short hair. But it's different for transgender girls. I *need* long hair." Her mother acknowledges that it is indeed different. Her mother wants to make it right, but doesn't know how. Trinity's brother, Aiden, suggests a wig, but at the beauty store, Trinity's mom notes that Trinity is "a beautiful Black girl and her curly hair is *already* perfect. None of these feel right." This gives Aiden another idea: "Trinity needs her own rainbow!" he exclaims. After picking out a variety of hair extensions, Trinity's mother stays up all night lovingly stitching the kaleido-

scope of colors into a wig that feels true to all aspects of Trinity's identity.

As children's books featuring transgender characters first started coming out, they exclusively featured transgender children. While genderqueer children need to see themselves in books (and cisgender children need to get to know these characters as well), they also need to see positive adult role models who are genderqueer. Plus, children in our communities likely have important adults in their lives who are transgender — a family member, a teacher, a neighbor, a coach. Gayle E. Pitman's *My Maddy* is an important title that I include in my repertoire of diverse family stories though it is not written by a trans author. A loving family story about a girl whose parent is nonbinary, *My Maddy* beautifully fills the need for stories of transgender adults for young people. The young, white protagonist does not refer to her parent as her daddy or her mommy, but rather as her motorcycle-riding, spork-loving, hazel-eyed Maddy, who shows her, and us, that "some of the best things in the world are not one thing or the other, but in between, and kind of both, and something entirely fantastically their own." This book is perfect for elementary-age students, and fits beautifully into classroom readings and discussions about what makes each of us and each of our families special.

PICTURE BOOK BIOGRAPHIES

Reading picture book biographies by and about trans people to students is another fantastic way to introduce students to positive role models. Since the publication of *I Am Jazz* in 2014, more biographies and histories of LGBTQ+ people, including transgender and genderqueer people, have been published. Two powerful new picture books based on real people show how two performers — one Hawaiian and one Rajasthani — find belonging in dancing outside of the gender binary. In *Hoʻonani Hula Warrior*, a young, Native Hawaiian child, Hoʻonani, learns that the high school kāne (males) will perform a traditional hula chant. Hoʻonani imagines herself leading the chant, "If only she were kāne AND old enough for high school." Her teacher, Kumu Hina, a Hawaiian cultural practitioner, community leader, and trans activist, encourages Hoʻonani to audition. When her sister asks, "Why do you always have to reject wahine things?" Hoʻonani answers, "Just because I feel more kāne doesn't mean I'm not wahine! I'm in the middle! Why can't you let me be?" Hoʻonani, who feels "Strong, sure, and steady" in herself, ultimately finds acceptance from her classmates and her entire family when leading the traditional hula chant.

Similarly, in *Desert Queen*, based on drag performer Queen Harish, Harish Kumar experienced both ridicule and encouragement in his journey to becoming the "Whirling Desert Queen of Rajasthan." In gorgeously detailed and brilliantly colorful illustrations inspired by Jaisalmer's cultural heritage, readers witness Harish's transformation, "The boy is shiny and glittery and NEW." Svabhu Kohli's stunning illustrations and Jyoti Rajan Gopal's sparse poems balance each other to bring Queen Harish to life:

> And . . . not-so-suddenly
> and after a much longer time
> than was right . . .
> The dancer is seen . . .
> SEEN.
>
> Not
> Boy OR girl.
> Man OR woman.
>
> But
> fluid
> flowing
> like a dance
> in between
> and all around.
>
> No more hiding.
> No more lines in the
> sand.
>
> Because
> He is She
> She is He
> and BOTH
> are the DESERT QUEEN.

A wonderful collective LGBTQ+ biography for elementary-age students is *Kind Like Marsha: Learning from LGBTQ+ Leaders* by Sarah Prager, which features both historical and contemporary transgender activists such as Marsha P. Johnson, an African American gay liberation activist who along with Puerto Rican-Venezuelan-American trans advocate Sylvia Rivera helped lead the Stonewall uprising, and X. González, a Cuban American gun control advocate and queer rights activist. Simple statements such as "Be Kind like Marsha," "Be Determined like Sylvia," or "Be Outspoken like X," along with the brief biography of each leader, make this an excellent book for younger elementary-age students, or a springboard for further research by older students.

Teachers who want to provide a more detailed, though still brief, introduction to trans leaders in U.S. history, should check out another fabulous resource for older elementary-age students: *Be Amazing: A History of Pride*. The colorful illustrations and glittery cover by Dylan Glynn catches readers' eyes sparking curiosity. With clear, succinct, and powerful writing, trans advocate, author, performer, model, and former child drag sensation Desmond Napoles (aka Desmond is Amazing) shares important people and moments in LGBTQ+ history, noting at the opening of the book that "I can be myself thanks to my parents, who let me be me . . . and thanks to the very brave people who fought to make it okay for me, or anyone like me, to be whoever we want to be."

INFORMATIONAL TEXTS

Whether I am reading stories about families with 1st graders, exploring biographies about change makers with 2nd graders, or looking at representation in children's literature with 3rd graders, if I need a nonfiction title to help elementary-age children discuss gender and gender identity, my go-to book is *It Feels Good to Be Yourself: A Book About Gender Identity*. In an author's note at the end of the book, Theresa Thorn writes, "My daughter's gender identity and expression are personal and unique to her; they have very little to do with me or my opinions, assumptions, and preconceptions. I wanted to give my daughter a book in which she could see herself. A book that reflected her back without judgment. I wanted, further, to give that experience to all kids." With Theresa Thorn's straightforward and inclusive writing, and Noah Grigni's gorgeously colorful and inclusive illustrations, the pair have done just that. *It Feels Good to Be Yourself* is an accessible resource for elementary-age students, teachers, and families that leaves open a pathway to possibilities noting "Just like there are many different ways to be a boy or a girl, there are many different ways to be nonbinary — too many to fit in a book! . . . And even with all these possible ways to be, some kids don't feel any of the words they know fit them exactly right. There are a never-ending number of ways to be yourself in the world."

Another amazing nonfiction resource for parents, educators, and older students is *Seeing Gender: An Illustrated Guide to Identity and Expression* by Iris Gottlieb. Combining simple illustrations, clear writing, fascinating facts, short biographies, and straightforward definitions, Iris Gottlieb provides a plethora of short essays and explanations on a wide range of topics that could be used with a wide range of age groups. For

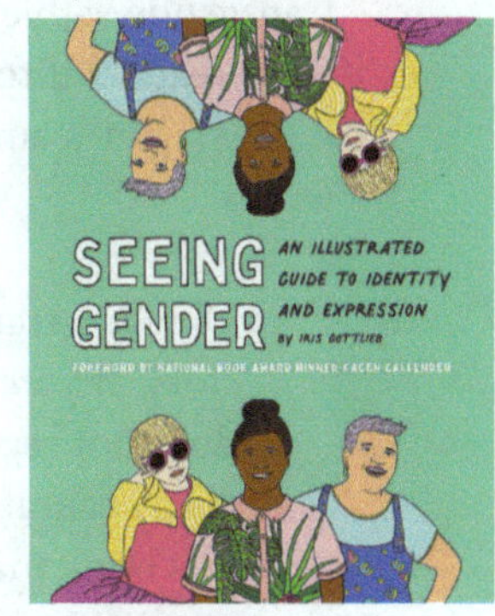

example, Gottlieb's essays and illustrations on "Gender Identity," "Gender Expression," and "1800's Clothing" could be used by a parent or educator working with elementary-age students to spark discussion about gender as a social construct. Other essays, however, contain more mature content that may be better suited for teens and adults.

In the introduction, Meredith Talusan reminds us that "We 'see' gender all the time — or at least our made up perception of gender. It's often something we forget we created, even though it exerts a great deal of influence over our lives." Talusan also reminds us that this book "is not just for trans people and nonbinary people, but for anyone who has a relationship with gender, which means everyone you know, including you."

The same is true for all of these books, whether picture books or problem novels, these books are for anyone of any gender.

MIDDLE GRADE FICTION

In the world of middle grade fiction, we see more and more trans literature as well. Many titles are still "problem novels" where the protagonist faces prejudice and bullying because of their gender identity. However, three things stand out about these newer titles: almost all are written by transgender and nonbinary writers providing role models in both the book's characters and the book's author; they all feature peers and adults who support the trans character as they deal with other people's prejudice; and they all stretch beyond realistic fiction into other genres. It's important to include these powerful problem novels in classrooms and libraries. Not only do they reflect what is tragically still a realistic experience, but they also offer hope.

MIDDLE GRADE SPORTS FICTION

Three titles that most closely connect to realistic fiction, and that tie in directly with current legislative issues, are three sports fiction titles written by three transgender or genderqueer athletes. *Obie Is Man Enough*, by Schuyler Bailar, the first transgender athlete to compete in any sport on an NCAA Division I men's team, takes readers through a Korean American swimmer's first season competing with a new swim team and competing as a boy. In a note to readers, Schuyler Bailar writes:

> Obie is a transgender boy who experiences transphobia throughout the story. If you are not transgender, please recognize that this transphobia does not represent all hatred and discrimination we experience. Still, it is an accurate representation that some experience. Certain moments in this book may be difficult to read for those who have experienced similar discrimination. Please take care of yourself as you read, especially if you are also transgender.

This compassionate, clear writing carries through the entire novel. While there are very painful scenes — particularly involving Obie's former coach and his former best friend — there are also tender scenes, loads of support, and tons of encouragement from Obie's family and his peers. Particularly poignant is the camaraderie and support Obie gets from two of his new teammates and friends, Mikey and Pooch. Whether Mikey and Pooch are accompanying Obie as he tries on his first boys' high-tech fast suit, standing up for him in the locker room, or rooting for him poolside, readers will cheer for Obie right alongside them.

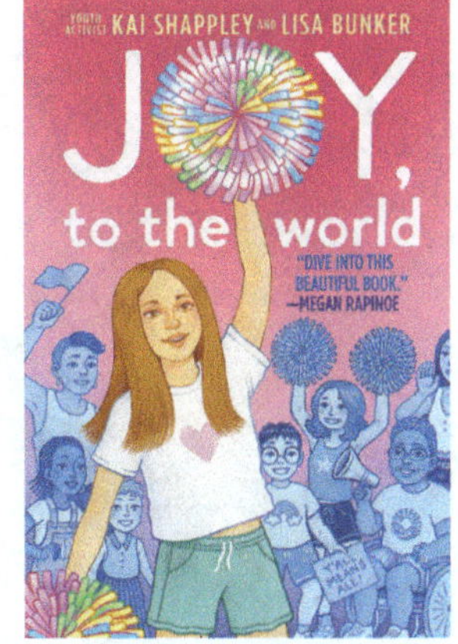

And on the topic of cheering, *Joy to the World* follows Joy, a young white girl who falls in love with cheerleading after moving to Texas. She is thrilled to make the middle school cheer squad, but her delight quickly turns to despair after she is kicked off the team because someone outs her for being trans. Joy turns her despair into determination, after learning about activist and actress Kai Shappley, who co-wrote the book with Lisa Bunker, author of *Zenobia July*. In her fight against the school board, Joy faces challenges and finds friends and family. Inspired by Kai Shappley's own experience as an activist standing up to Texas legislators from a young age, *Joy to the World* offers a glimpse into an experience both relatable and uniquely shaped by Joy's many identities — white, transgender girl, athlete, Christian, Texan. *Joy to the World* provides two role models with unique stories of transitioning: Kai Shappley standing up to Texas politicians as a kindergartner and Lisa Bunker transitioning as an older adult and then being elected to the New Hampshire state legislature.

The above two titles both feature athletes who have already transitioned. A. J. Sass' novel *Ana on the Edge* features a Chinese Jewish girl whose growing understanding of her own gender doesn't line up with the gender binary of her beloved sport, figure skating. Ana is torn between internal pressure to stick to the expensive choreography that her mother worked hard to pay for and the deep knowing that the princess-themed music, costume, and choreography do not reflect who she is. When a new student thinks she's a boy, Ana doesn't correct him, enjoying for a time the newness of trying on male pronouns. Through many spins and falls, both on and off the ice, Ana ultimately finds her way. For Ana, what's more important than pronouns is being true to all the parts of who she is: "I'm not sure when I'll absolutely know if I fall in between a boy and a girl or outside that binary entirely. . . . And that's fine. Uncertainty feels like less of a burden and more of an opportunity. I am Ana. And Ana is I. I'm done being anyone but me."

MIDDLE GRADE REALISTIC FICTION

Another realistic fiction novel by A. J. Sass worthy of attention is *Ellen Outside the Lines*. Ellen is a white, Jewish, 13-year-old autistic cisgender lesbian who has to navigate a new city and a last-minute change from classroom instruction to experiential scavenger hunt on her class trip to Barcelona. The intersection of these identities is important as they impact Ellen's everyday life and experience, including her ability to understand a new classmate and friend's gender fluidity: "Thinking of Isa as they, them, and their hasn't been hard, even if I don't get how to fit them into my diary's pronouns category. But knowing what Isa meant when they said they're not a boy or a girl? That part is like our scavenger hunt clue: I understand each word on its own but not what it means as a whole." Though Isa is not the main character of this book, they are a significant character. Ellen's authenticity as she tries to understand her friend who does not fit into Ellen's binary, black-and-white thinking, creates compassion for both Isa and Ellen. If you know any readers who love a good travel/adventure/romance, or someone trying to better understand gender fluidity, this is a fantastic choice.

Similarly, if you know a reader who loves a good romance, can't resist a sweet dog story, or who needs support in better understanding gender norms and gender fluidity — whether their own or someone else's — *Both Can Be True* by Jules Machias is an excellent choice. Told in alternating chapters, Daniel and Ash work together to save a dog's life. At the same time, they are each struggling with ideas about gender that restrict who they are. Daniel is a white cisgender male who battles both his own and others' definitions of masculinity and opinions about his deeply felt and openly expressed emotions. Ash, a white classmate who moves between male and female, also faces internal and external judgment about who they are. What's so beautiful about their stories is the way their paths — so seemingly different at first — intertwine in a beautiful blend of self-awareness, acceptance, mutual understanding, and affection.

In a presentation at David Douglas High School in Portland, Oregon, author Cynthia Leitich Smith discussed a repeating pattern in children's literature: When books are first published by/about a marginalized group of people, the first books published are realistic historical fiction centered on landmark figures/events, problem novels and picture books highlighting core cultural elements (food, clothing, holidays), and then on struggles with power structures relating to that group's identity. Over time, more books get published in other genres: everyday life historical fiction, biography of lesser-known figures, and contemporary stories that are not centered on challenges relating to the character's identity. But the last genre of books written by/about people from this shared identity that finally get published is speculative fiction — science fiction and fantasy.

MIDDLE GRADE FANTASY

A powerful middle grade novel that reaches into the realm of fantasy is Mark Oshiro's *The Insiders*. When 12-year-old Héctor Muñoz moves from San Francisco to a small town in the California Central Valley, he feels confident that he will make new friends who welcome him for who he is — an outgoing, musical theater- and fashion-loving Mexican American kid who is openly gay. Instead, he's met with a distressingly nightmarish response — a white classmate who is a ruthless homophobic bully, and a cruel white teacher who only sees who she thinks Héctor is and who harshly punishes him for it. Héctor makes a few "friends," but they are too frightened and intimidated to stand up for him, at least initially. Though Héctor's parents and abuela fully love and support him, Héctor doesn't feel he can tell them what is going on. His only refuge is the janitor's closet that turns out to be a magic portal that connects him to two other students from across the country — one an African American lesbian who faces her own homophobic school administrator, and the other a nonbinary white boy who feels no one understands them so everyone simply ignores them. *The Insiders* beautifully, and painfully, explores the intersection of race, sexuality, gender, and class, highlighting how a person's biases can blind them from truly seeing a child — whether that's seeing the school bully or seeing a shining star. Though the bullying by both students and school personnel is intense, *The Insiders* ultimately delivers hope when quite literally the spotlight shows the truth of who the bullies and who the heroes really are.

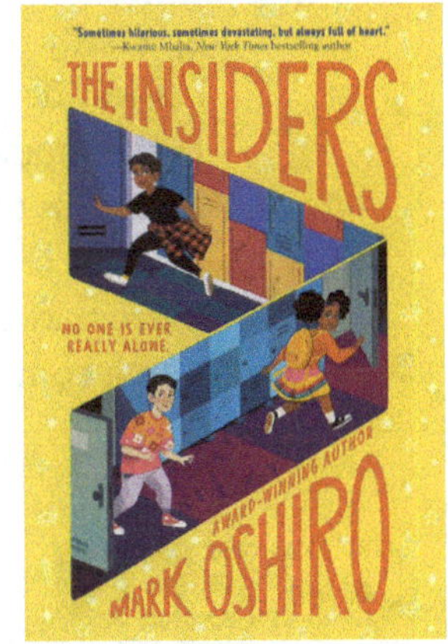

In addition to fantasy being the final genre where emerging voices are published, another milestone in publishing is when we start seeing stories of everyday life, of joy, and of celebration. Kyle Lukoff manages to do both, bringing a bit of the paranormal into a much more positive reality in his ghostly novel *Too Bright to See*. Bug, a white child whose beloved uncle recently died, is about to start middle school and Bug's best friend, Moira, has very specific ideas about what they both need to do to get ready: figure out fashion, learn to put on makeup, and talk about cute boys. None of those things are on Bug's list, though. A new ghost is haunting Bug's rickety country home, and while Bug has always felt comfortable with the ghosts that reside in the house, this ghost is different. This ghost seems determined to deliver a message to Bug. Is Bug brave enough to face the truth? When I read *Too Bright to See*, what excited me more than Kyle Lukoff writing a ghost story with a trans character, was Kyle Lukoff writing a coming out story where the trans character is so fully supported, loved, and accepted for being who they are. It felt as if Kyle Lukoff were writing the reality he wished to create.

MIDDLE GRADE STORIES OF JOY

Alex Gino certainly did that with their newest novel *Green*. A companion book to *Melissa* and *Rick*, Alex Gino opens the novel with the following dedication: "For us, because we all deserve joyful communities." The first chapter is an affirmation of a reality that all our students deserve:

> Green's life was pretty great, especially for a kid in middle school. They were queer and nonbinary, and had lots of queer and trans friends. Pretty much everyone used their name and pronouns, and they felt mostly comfortable with their body the way it was. They didn't have a nemesis or a bully or anything like that, and most of their teachers were at least halfway decent, if not rather good. Their family was small, just them and Dad at home, but Dad was way closer to awesome than awful. Yep, the going was sweet for Green Gibson.

Green may solidly reside on the realistic fiction shelf, but that opening is pure magic. In a community in which Green, a white, gender-fluid middle school student, is so fully seen and supported, it's no surprise that the problem in this problem novel is not about Green searching for acceptance from family, friends, or themself. They openly, if a bit awkwardly, tell their dad when they get their first period. They have multiple friends, including their peers in their school's Rainbow Spectrum group, plus multiple teachers who both learn from and advocate for them. And while Green isn't sure how they feel about their period starting, they treat themself with compassion and acceptance, realizing most cisgender kids probably aren't sure how they feel about their bodies changing either. As Green tries to process what puberty means to them, and what their options are, they do some research:

> Green had done a little more reading about hormone blockers. They would stop your period, but they would also stop your body from developing in other ways, and Green couldn't say for sure that they wanted that. They enjoyed the small curves they were starting to see on their body, and they didn't necessarily want those to stop.

Instead of the previous plot points of early trans lit problem novels, *Green* is about a kid getting their first period and having their first crush. It's a tender story of family, friendship, and first love. It's a story about a kid living their beautiful, complicated life. Can you imagine a world in which every child is so fully supported and seen, both by their community and by themself? *Green* is full of such tenderness with a satisfyingly sweet ending, but perhaps the most magical thing about Alex Gino's *Green* is that it feels like it could be real.

When I think back to 2018 and the debate swirling around *Melissa*, I remember the hope I felt any time I found a book featuring a transgender character. Yes, there is a long history of trans lit for adults, but finding children's books with trans characters was not easy. Finding books as powerful and relatable as Melissa felt like triumph. Still, in 2018, I had only two picture books and five middle grade novels with trans characters in my school library, and only two of those titles were written by a transgender person. In contrast, I now have multiple picture books, nonfiction books, and middle grade titles by multiple transgender or genderqueer authors, among them Kyle Lukoff, A. J. Sass, Jenn Reese, Lisa Bunker, and, of course, Alex Gino. This shift in the sheer number, depth, and beauty of trans literature for children gives me hope that . . .

> after a much longer time
> than was right . . .
> The child is seen . . .
> SEEN.

Lora Lyn Worden (she/her) is an elementary school librarian in Portland, Oregon.

American Library Association. 2024. Top 13 Books of 2013. www.ala.org

Bailar, Schuyler. 2021. *Obie is Man Enough.* Crown Books for Young Readers.

Gale, Heather. 2019. *Hoʻonani: Hula Warrior.* Tundra Books.

Gino, Alex. 2024. *Green.* Scholastic Press.

Gino, Alex. 2015. *Melissa.* Scholastic Press.

Gopal, Jyoti Rajan. 2023. *Desert Queen.* Levine Querido.

Herthel, Jessica, and Jennings, Jazz. 2014. *I Am Jazz.* Dial Books.

Lukoff, Kyle. 2021. *Too Bright to See.* Dial Books for Young Readers.

Lukoff, Kyle. 2019. *When Aidan Became a Brother.* Lee & Low Books.

Machias, Jules. 2022. *Both Can Be True.* Quill Tree Books.

Napoles, Desmond. 2020. *Be Amazing: A History of Pride.*

Neal, DeShanna, and Neal, Trinity. 2020. *My Rainbow.* Kokila.

Oshiro, Mark. 2021. *The Insiders.* HarperCollins.

Pitman, Gayle E. 2020. *My Maddy.* American Psychological Association.

Prager, Sarah. 2022. *Kind Like Marsha: Learning from LGBTQ+ Leaders.* Running Press Kids.

Reese, Jenn. 2022. *Every Bird a Prince.* Henry Holt and Company.

Sass, A. J. 2021. *Ana on the Edge.* Little, Brown Books for Young Readers.

Sass, A. J. 2022. *Ellen Outside the Lines.* Little, Brown and Company.

Schulman, Melissa. 2023. Q & A with Ami Polonsky. *Publishers Weekly.* www.publishersweekly.com/pw/by-topic/childrens/childrens-authors/article/91265-q-a-with-ami-polonsky.html

Shappley, Kai, and Bunker, Lisa. 2023. *Joy to the World.* Clarion Books.

Smith, Cynthia Leitich. 2023. *Native American Cultural Night* at David Douglas High School.

Thorn, Theresa. 2019. *It Feels Good to Be Yourself: A Book About Gender Identity.* Henry Holt and Co.

The Trevor Project. 2022. 2022 National Survey on LGBTQ Youth Mental Health. www.thetrevorproject.org/survey-2022/

The Trevor Project. 2023. 2023 U.S. National Survey on the Mental Health of LGBTQ Young People. www.thetrevorproject.org/survey-2023/

The Trevor Project. 2021. Facts About Suicide Among LGBTQ+ Young People. www.thetrevorproject.org/resources/article/facts-about-lgbtq-youth-suicide/

ADDITIONAL RESOURCES

ORGANIZATIONS

Transgender Law Center
transgenderlawcenter.org
The Transgender Law Center is the largest U.S. transgender-led civil rights organization. Their work includes legal services, and support for trans people with a variety of intersectional identities such as trans people with disabilities, trans people of color, and trans youth leaders.

National Center for Transgender Equality
transequality.org
The National Center for Transgender Equality advocates to change policies and society to increase understanding and acceptance of transgender people. NCTE provides a variety of self-help resources from navigating legal ID and name changes to Know Your Rights resources for settings from schools to airport security.

TGI Justice Project
tgijp.org
TGIJP challenges the human rights abuses committed against transgender, gender variant, and intersex people in prisons, jails, detention centers, and beyond. (California)

Trans Justice Funding Project
transjusticefundingproject.org
TJFP supports grassroots, trans justice groups run by and for trans people in the United States, including U.S. territories.

GUIDES TO TRANS-AFFIRMING LAWS

The National Center for Transgender Equality has a student-friendly guide to how Title IX can be interpreted to protect trans students, as well as FERPA, to support students in school. transequality.org/know-your-rights/schools

Harvard Law School's LGBTQIA+ Advocacy Clinic created a Trans Youth Handbook in 2020 that covers trans youth rights, not just at school but also work and health care: hlslgbtq.org/trans-youth-handbook

The Human Rights Campaign's "Welcoming Schools" resource includes an updated list of the federal laws and constitutional rights that affirm transgender students: welcomingschools.org/resources/faq-on-supporting-transgender-and-non-binary-students-in-k-12-schools

GUIDES FOR SCHOOL ADMINISTRATORS AND PARENTS

The Oregon Department of Education has released a 2023 report called Supporting Gender Expansive Students: Guidance for Schools, which can be used to assist districts looking to implement more affirming policies. oregon.gov/ode/students-and-family/equity/civilrights/Documents/ODE-Supporting-Gender-Expansive-Students.pdf

The Human Rights Campaign released in 2020 the "A Parent's Quick Guide for In-School Transitions," which offers support for parents of gender-expansive children, as well as suggested professional development for teachers. hrc.org/resources/a-parents-quick-guide-for-in-school-transitions-empowering-families-and-schools-to-support-transgender-and-non-binary-students

Lambda Legal offers guidance on how to change school records to reflect affirmed names: legacy.lambdalegal.org/know-your-rights/article/youth-ferpa-faq

TRANSGENDER HISTORY AND CURRICULUM RESOURCES

Digital Transgender Archive
digitaltransgenderarchive.net
This digital archive contains primary sources and resource sets from pre-colonial ideas of gender through transgender feminism.

Rights, Respect, Responsibility Curriculum
3rs.org
Advocates for Youth has published a free comprehensive sexual health education

curriculum that affirms LGBTQIA community, and includes resources for schools experiencing backlash for using affirming curriculum.

MENTAL HEALTH SUPPORT FOR TRANS STUDENTS

Trans Lifeline
translifeline.org | Call (877) 565-8860
The Trans Lifeline provides a peer support hotline run by and for trans people.

Trevor Project
thetrevorproject.org | Call 866-488-7386 or text 678-678
The Trevor Project provides a hotline for LGBTQIA youth 13–24 for crisis intervention and suicide prevention.

ACKNOWLEDGEMENTS

This book is for trans students, for those whose survival we fight for and for those who have not survived. We offer this book in honor of the visionary trans leaders who remind us how much these stories need to be told, who have shown us both power and self-love — from Marsha P. Johnson, Miss Major, Janet Mock, Laverne Cox, Chelsea Manning, Chase Strangio, Sarah McBride, Danica Roem, and so many more. Their legacies live on in the words and work of all the contributors to this book and those who take these lessons back to their classrooms, schools, and districts. We are lucky to fight alongside each of you for trans liberation.

Many of the essays in this book first appeared in *Rethinking Schools* and were improved by the magazine's rigorous editorial process. The staff and editors of *Rethinking Schools* — Wayne Au, Elizabeth Barbian, Bill Bigelow, Ari Bloomekatz, Grace Cornell Gonzales, Jesse Hagopian, Aubrey Hogan, Cierra Kaler-Jones, Stan Karp, David Levine, Larry Miller, Gina Palazzari, Bob Peterson, Adam Sanchez, Lindsay Stevens, Dyan Watson, Ursula Wolfe-Rocca, Moé Yonamine, Missy Zombor — scrutinized every article, making all of us better writers and teachers in the process. For any book to hit the shelves, invisible hands make the impossible possible. This publication might not have ever made it past our imaginations if it hadn't been for Bill Bigelow, who brought to the book not only his capacity as an editor, but also his knowledge as a teacher, which helped us hone articles' language, politics, and lessons. Nancy Zucker endowed the book with her artistic and poetic sensibility, seeking trans artists whose visions matched the intention of the book. Throughout this writing, editing, visioning process, Nancy was a total partner in the work, putting up with us when we changed our minds, challenging us to see the book beyond the words. As always, Lawrence Sanfilippo was our proofreader extraordinaire. Cierra Kaler-Jones, Rethinking Schools executive director, deserves credit for lining up funding and resources, as well as the willpower to move this book to the finish line.

Linda writes:
When our youngest child, Gretchen, was in elementary school, she/they became Tommy at home. She/they loved Robin Hood, not Maid Marian, *Little Men*, not *Little Women*. At the time, we didn't have the language for nonbinary or transgender, but over the past 40 years, she/they have been our kind and persistent tutor. During our Oregon Writing Project (OWP) writing retreats, OWP coaches Mykhiel Deych and Ty Marshall birthed new consciousness for everyone in our group with powerful stories about the emotional burden of exclusionary practices for trans students and teachers. After reading *Melissa* (formerly published as *George*), our grandson Xavier taught me that with even a little education, children can effortlessly transition out of a binary understanding of the world, embracing a fuller range of humanity.

Ty writes:
This book would not exist without Linda, who has gathered so many amazing teacher leaders around her dining room table and cheered on so many brilliant words waiting to be heard. I entered this project from that same table, crying in despair over my struggles in my classroom, and left that table with a lifeline and a thread of hope — to gather stories of other trans teachers and students and edit them into the book you are now holding. Thanks for believing in all of us so much. Thanks to my partner Mykhiel Deych for showing me the searing power of writing and art as central in our fight for justice, and also for reminding me about all the ways we are worth more than just our productivity, and to Zorya, Malachi, and Misha for making us a family! Thanks to V, for demanding bravery and visibility, and to all my fellow teachers (and students!) trying to plant the seeds of a better world inside the old.

INDEX

G

H

I

J

K

L

Q

R

S

T

U

V

W

X

Z

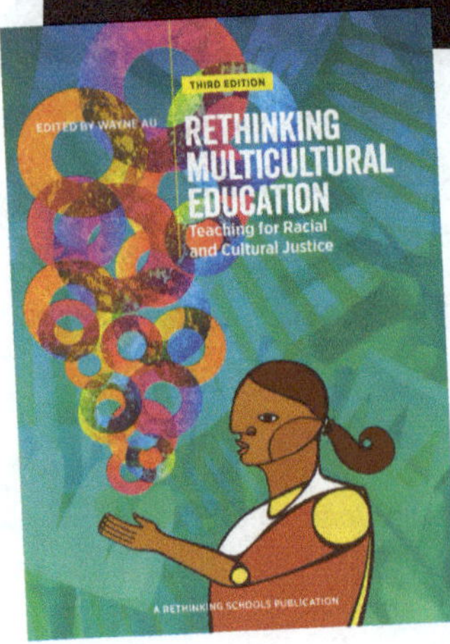

Rethinking Multicultural Education

Teaching for Racial and Cultural Justice

Edited by Wayne Au

This new and expanded third edition demonstrates a powerful vision of anti-racist, social justice education. Practical, rich in story, and analytically sharp, ***Rethinking Multicultural Education*** reclaims multicultural education as part of a larger struggle for justice and against racism, colonization, and cultural oppression—in schools and society.

Paperback • 418 pages • ISBN: 978-0-942961-53-9

$24.95*

Teaching for Black Lives

Edited by Dyan Watson, Jesse Hagopian, Wayne Au

Teaching for Black Lives grows directly out of the movement for Black lives. We recognize that anti-Black racism constructs Black people, and Blackness generally, as not counting as human life. Throughout this book, we provide resources and demonstrate how teachers can connect curriculum to young people's lives and root their concerns and daily experiences in what is taught and how classrooms are set up. We also highlight the hope and beauty of student activism and collective action.

Paperback • 368 pages • ISBN: 978-0-942961-04-1

$29.95*

Rethinking Sexism, Gender, and Sexuality

Edited by Kim Cosier, Rachel L. S. Harper, Jeff Sapp, Jody Sokolower, and Melissa Bollow Tempel

There has never been a more important time for students to understand sexism, gender, and sexuality—or to make schools nurturing places for all of us. The thought-provoking articles and curriculum in this life-changing book will be invaluable to everyone who wants to address these issues in their classroom, school, home, and community.

Paperback • 400 pages • ISBN: 978-0-942961-59-1

$24.95*

eBook and Kindle: $9.95: rethinkingschools.org/RSGS

Teacher Unions and Social Justice

Organizing for the schools and communities our students deserve

Edited By Michael Charney, Jesse Hagopian, and Bob Peterson

An anthology of over 60 articles documenting the history and the how-tos of social justice unionism. Together, they describe the growing movement to forge multiracial alliances with communities to defend and transform public education.

Paperback • 448 pages • ISBN: 978-0-942961-09-6

$29.95

The New Teacher Book THIRD EDITION

Finding purpose, balance, and hope during your first years in the classroom

Edited by Linda Christensen, Stan Karp, Bob Peterson, and Moé Yonamine

THIRD EDITION • FULLY REVISED •

Teaching is a lifelong challenge, but the first few years in the classroom are typically the hardest. This expanded third edition of ***The New Teacher Book*** grew out of Rethinking Schools workshops with early-career teachers. It offers practical guidance on how to flourish in schools and classrooms and connect in meaningful ways with students and families from all cultures and backgrounds.

Paperback • 352 pages • 978-0-942961-03-4

$24.95

Reading, Writing, and Rising Up

SECOND EDITION

Teaching About Social Justice and the Power of the Written Word

By Linda Christensen

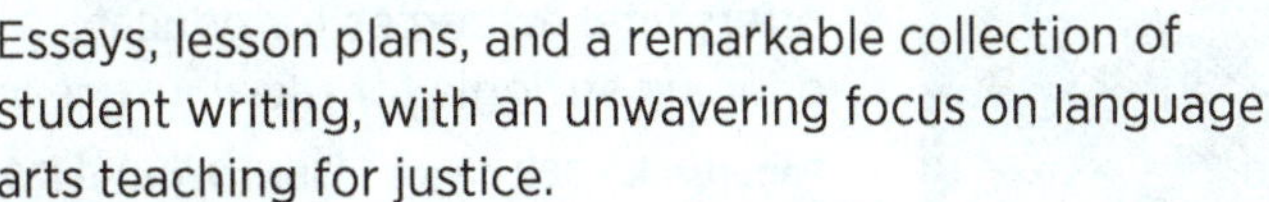
Essays, lesson plans, and a remarkable collection of student writing, with an unwavering focus on language arts teaching for justice.

Paperback • 196 pages • ISBN: 978-0-942961-69-0

$24.95*